PATH TO THE LIGHT

Kabbalah Centre Publishing is a registered DBA of
Kabbalah Centre International, Inc.

For further information:

The Kabbalah Centre
155 E. 48th St., New York, NY 10017
1062 S. Robertson Blvd., Los Angeles, CA 90035

1.800.Kabbalah www.kabbalah.com

Printed in USA, December 2019

ISBN: 978-1-57189-981-1

eBook ISBN: 978-1-57189-983-5

Design: HL Design (Hyun Min Lee) www.hldesignco.com

PATH TO THE LIGHT

KABBALAH CENTRE PUBLISHING

DECODING THE BIBLE WITH KABBALAH

An Anthology
of Commentary
from Kabbalist
Rav Berg

**BOOK OF
SHEMOT
Volume 5**

**Shemot
Va'era
Bo
Beshalach**

May the wisdom of Kabbalah that Rav Berg shares in this
book open people's hearts to experience a greater
connection to the Light of the Creator and
the Light of their soul.

May this wisdom bring those, whose soul mate
connection has not yet manifested itself, to a union with
the other half of their soul for eternity.

Itzhak Ben Leizer Chaim

PREFACE

Path to the Light, Shemot, Volume 5, contains Rav Berg's commentary of the portions Shemot, Va'era, Bo, and Beshalach. Those of us who feel certain we know these sections relate the story of Moses leading the Israelites out of Egypt, through the wilderness, and eventually to the Promised Land of Israel are swiftly disabused of such certitude. As always, the Rav is quick to point out how invaluable a tool the Zohar is in the correction of misconceptions, contradictions, and the sheer nonsense we encounter by taking the Bible literally.

Here, we receive guidance from the sages of the Zohar: "Rav Aba opened the discussion TO BRING PROOF TO HIS WORDS saying: "Come and behold the works of the Lord who has made desolations (Heb. shamot) on the Earth." (Psalms 46:9) Do not pronounce it shamot but rather shemot (lit. "names")." Just these 36 words demonstrate the awesome shifts in our perception of meaning in the Torah provided by Rav Berg's matchless erudition and skillful use of the kabbalistic tools—those instruments of vision and assistance given to us by the Zohar.

The following text is an amalgam of discourses on this topic delivered by the Rav over many years. It shows plainly the relentless consistency evident over half a century in Rav Berg's unravelling of the more perplexing biblical mysteries. The Rav's style is disarmingly simple and straightforward, with metaphors, similes, and analogies taken from everyday life deployed in an illuminating manner to reveal some of the most profound thoughts a human mind is capable of grasping. But in no way is this a dry, scholarly work of exegesis. Lest any reader mistake his unwavering purpose, the Rav frequently reminds us that Kabbalah is not about the amassing of information. "It is rather," he says, "a technology that supports the improvement of human life here and now."

And for those readers who may have even a suspicion that Kabbalah is a religion, the Rav makes it definitively clear in his commentary that this is not the case. He does this by delineating the function of, and benefit of, this wisdom to both individuals and the planet as a whole.

Most, if not all of us, have Bible passages we find difficult to understand or reason. A number of these problematic sections appear in the Book of Shemot, and the reader might be relieved to find that the Rav sympathizes with their frustration. Many times we find him saying, "Why do we need to know this?" or "What use is this information today?" Those familiar with the Rav's discursive manner, however, will know he asks questions only to answer them.

It is a central tenet in the Rav's teachings that the Bible is not a charming, if at times dreadfully inconsistent history about ancient peoples and their atavistic ways. Rather it is eternally vital and relevant wisdom regarding what is perhaps the greatest of all human questions: What is the point and purpose of our lives? For those anxious to have this question answered, as well as for those who have not yet realized they need to ask it, this commentary will come as a momentous revelation.

Indeed, assembled herein, there are many examples of the Rav's insights that will enlighten all who now question fretfully what the future holds for us in a world consumed by chaos, uncertainty, and fear. When tackling the more baffling areas of scripture, the Rav always remains on message, and he never shies away from those issues that plague all of humankind. If God is good, why does one become sick with cancer? How can we neutralize the effects of our past negative or destructive actions? What is a soul? How can we shield ourselves from all the chaos and wickedness that surround us? For those who ask these and a thousand other seemingly unanswerable questions, all of them at the crucial core of human existence, the following pages will be as vivifying as spring rain.

As the Creator promised, we are not abandoned here alone without a guide or any help. The guidebook is now in our hands, and it contains all the help anyone could ask for—all the help, and then still more. The greatest secret to be revealed is that regarding the Lightforce of God, whose nature is wholly positive and purely beneficent. This is the embodiment of that Lightforce. It is Love in action.

The preface in this volume, and all those found in Path to the Light, Beresheet, Volumes 1-4, were written by the late Paul William Roberts. He has been a friend of the Kabbalah Centre for two decades and in that time has contributed to the publishing department on many editorial projects.

Paul was educated at Exeter College, University of Oxford in England, which was founded in 1314 as a school to educate clergyman. He passed away in May, 2019.

He will be missed.

TABLE OF CONTENTS

BOOK OF SHEMOT:

Portion of Shemot

PORTION OF SHEMOT

The second book of the Five Books of Moses is the Book of *Shemot*. The Hebrew word shemot means "names;" yet the word used as a title in the English translation of this second book of the Bible is "exodus." Also, the first portion of each book of the Bible is always called by the same name as the entire book. For example, the first portion of the Book of Beresheet is "Beresheet;" the first portion of the Book of Shemot is "Shemot," and so on.

The first of the Five Books of Moses in English translations is called Genesis (Beresheet), meaning "in the beginning," and this first portion describes Creation. So how did the word *shemot* come to be translated as "exodus"? The majority of the second book of the Bible does not deal with an exodus at all, yet it is still called Exodus.

To help us understand, we will connect with the Zohar, which is the way we begin all of our discussions because when we read the Zohar we understand everything on another level of consciousness. It is that simple.

The Zohar says:

> Rav Aba opened the discussion TO BRING PROOF TO HIS WORDS saying: "Come and behold the works of the Lord who has made desolations (Heb. *shamot*) on the Earth." (Tehilim 46:9) Do not pronounce it *shamot*, but rather *shemot* (lit. "names"). This follows a similar thought expressed by Rabbi Chiya that, as the Holy One, blessed be He, has done in Heaven, so has He done on Earth. Just as there are Holy Names in Heaven, so are there Holy Names here on Earth. THESE ARE THE NAMES OF THE

TRIBES OF WHICH IT IS WRITTEN, "THESE ARE
THE NAMES OF THE CHILDREN OF ISRAEL…"
—Zohar, Shemot 8:53

From this passage in the Zohar we are told that this portion, and possibly the entire Book of Shemot, concerns names. Rav Shimon tells us this is referring to the 72 Names of God and other Holy Names. In other words, we are not talking solely about the names of the twelve tribes. Therefore, the Book of Shemot and the portion of Shemot do not address the actual exodus from Egypt but rather they deal with the matter that led to the exodus.

Why is it so important to discuss the matters that led to the exodus from Egypt? As we will learn shortly, no one could go out from Egypt. Only with the Lightforce of God were the Israelites able to depart. The Zohar explains that the Israelites would never have been freed had they not left at that time because they had reached the 49th Gate of Impurity. The Israelites who lived in Egypt did not want to leave as they were so enveloped by the force of Egypt— the Desire to Receive for the Self Alone. We know the Egyptians were masters of astrology, were able to construct pyramids, and to perform mummification. No other nation in the world had even a semblance of that kind of power. The Zohar says such power kept not only the Israelites but the entire world in bondage.

What is meant by the word "bondage"? Does it mean the slaves in Egypt were beaten and oppressed? This slavery is often presented as a Holocaust. Yet if we look through the verses of the Bible, the one thing the Israelites were in agreement about was that they wished to return to Egypt. Whenever they faced the slightest problem in the wilderness, their first outcry was to return. Could it really have been so bad in Egypt?

This entire Book of Shemot is not here to tell us a story of exodus because, if you read it superficially, the Israelites were unhappy to leave. In fact both the Midrash and the Zohar say that many Israelites died during the ninth plague of darkness because they did not really want to leave Egypt.

The Bible is a cosmic code, and not at all what it seems to be. The Zohar reveals what is behind the words. In this case, it is discussing an exodus that occurred 3,800 years ago. Of what concern is this for us today? We understand from Rav Shimon that the Bible cannot be treated as just a story book, or as something that contains the recitation of a heritage from our common past. The truth is that what happened 4,000 years ago is not very important to most of us. What matters is how this information can help us today in the here and now. If we remove the concealment of the portion of Shemot, and decipher the code, we will learn how to gain control over our destiny.

Both the Zohar and the Midrash say that never has there been a level of intelligence achieved as that possessed by the Generation of the Exodus. And, moreover, this level of intelligence will only exist again at the time of the coming of Messiah (*Mashiach*)—the generation we live in now. This level exists now because the souls alive today are all the souls of the Generation of the Exodus. We are the same ones who complained about not having water and eating *manna* in the desert—even after seeing all the miracles: the plagues, the bloody rivers, and the Splitting of the Red Sea. Who has the audacity to speak to God this way? The Zohar says that the people of the Time of the Coming of Messiah will be more audacious than any other people have ever been. The reason for these souls being incarnated with such audacity now is so that, this time around, they will complete their *tikkun* (spiritual correction).

More than half the Book of Shemot is devoted to the *Mishkan* (Tabernacle). What does the Tabernacle have to do with the exodus? The Tabernacle was the method by which the Israelites could tap the energy of the Lightforce of the Creator while they travelled in the wilderness. The Tabernacle is a preview of the Holy Temple in Jerusalem. It housed the Ark and the Holy of Holies. The Holy of Holies was where the Israelites could connect to all the energy existing in the cosmos. Energy is information, information is power; it is everything.

The portions in the Book of Shemot apply to all of humankind, and not simply to the children of Israel enslaved in Egypt. It is difficult to comprehend that this portion—a section that has been drawn out from the Upper Realms of the Creator—is accorded a translation that is furthest from the truth. There is no doubt that the Hebrew word *shemot* means "names," which, to our good fortune, applies to the 72 Names of God and other Holy Names we can access and apply.

The Zohar tells us that, just prior the splitting of the Red Sea, there was the revelation of the 72 Names of God through three biblical verses—Shemot 14:19-21. At that instant, nothing of a material substance could stand in the way of the Israelites, who could now rule everything in this universe because this power came. Up to this point, the Israelites did not have the 72 Names to allow them to make a connection. Herein lies the strength and knowledge by which we can control every part of the universe. If we can control the universe, maybe we can even control our destinies—which is what the Book of Shemot is really all about.

When we discuss Shemot, are we discussing history? Are we simply commemorating the fact that the Israelites came out of Egypt with a Seder during Passover? No, this is not the reason we participate in Passover. Passover is a cosmic time-frame, a moment when energy is available that can help us deal with our problems. The reason we study Shemot, and the reason Passover is important to us is not because of history or heritage. If I have one single goal in my life, it is to undo the notion that everything in the Bible deals with the past. There is no past or future—there is only now. It is not necessarily that things are bad right now, and that tomorrow is going to be better. What is our merit? What do we possess more of today than any previous generation has possessed? We are living in the Age of Aquarius, and for this reason we have the merit of this information so that maybe we will begin to understand and become rulers of our own lives.

The import of Shemot, as Rav Shimon bar Yochai tells us—and as Rashi also said, in his concealed way—is not that it details an exodus out of a country. As the Zohar asks so often, if reading this is merely part of celebrating or remembering, then what does it have to do with the present and with our personal situation?

It is for this reason that the sages of the Zohar revealed the concealed meaning of the Bible. As I repeat again, and indeed cannot repeat often enough, Rav Shimon said that anyone who considers the Bible on a superficial level is a fool—for this was never the intent of the Revelation on Mount Sinai. The Book of Shemot continues with the experience of Egypt as a place of chaos, pain, suffering, and cruel imprisonment. The Hebrew word for Egypt is *Mitzrayim*, [מצרים] which comes from the root word *metzar*, [מצר] meaning "to be closed in," and every other term for being confined.

Shemot 1:1 These are the names of the sons of Israel who came into Egypt with Jacob, each with his family: 2 Reuben, Simeon, Levi and Judah; 3 Issachar, Zebulun and Benjamin; 4 Dan and Naphtali; Gad and Asher. 5 And all the souls that were descendants of Jacob numbered seventy souls; Joseph was already in Egypt. 6 Now Joseph and all his brothers and all that generation died, 7 but the Israelites were fruitful and multiplied greatly and became exceedingly numerous, so that the land was filled with them.

Names in the Bible

The Zohar raises a question concerning the first verse of the portion of Shemot. The English translation says, "who *came* into Egypt," but the Hebrew word *haba'im* does not mean "came." In Hebrew, the word *ba'im* [באים] is not in a past tense but in the present tense—and it could almost be in a future tense. Did we not read in the previous portion that Jacob, Joseph and everyone died? So what does it mean that these are the names of the children of Israel who come into Egypt now? The Zohar also reminds us that the Bible begins by using the elevated name of Jacob, which is "Israel," then later again it uses the name Jacob.

How many times does the Bible have to tell us that the Israelites went into Egypt? In the Book of Beresheet, we were told that Jacob went down to Egypt—so what is the Bible indicating here? Viewed superficially, these verses do not make sense. We must look to the Zohar, which says that when the Israelites went into exile (*galut*) in Egypt, all the souls of the twelve tribes came and pleaded to the Upper Triad—Abraham, Isaac, and Jacob—saying, "How can you be so quiet when your children are going into exile? They will suffer all the retribution that could ever be given to one person or to any one nation." The Israelites needed all the assistance they could get because they were going to suffer extremes of retribution. When the Bible says "*came* into Egypt" it means that the souls of the twelve tribes came and pleaded at that time because this was the only way the Israelites could ever be redeemed. They needed an intervention. Therefore, the souls that *came* were not in a physical form because they had already died.

Shemot 1:5 says: "Joseph was already in Egypt." What does this mean? The previous portion told us that Joseph was already dead. The Zohar explains that the souls of Joseph, along with the other sons of Israel, never left Egypt because they knew that without the assistance of the twelve tribes the Israelites would never make it out of the country. The name "Jacob," and not that of "Israel," is used in this portion because "Jacob" does not represent the elevated state of consciousness or the Upper Triad. In the Upper Triad there is no chance of chaos, no chance of problems. Satan only exists in the Lower Triad. The name "Jacob" is used to indicate that the Israelites had to go down to the level of the Lower Triad. "Jacob" refers to the chaos. Rav Isaac Luria (the Ari) says these were the same souls of the Generation of the Flood and the Tower of Babel, and they had to reincarnate again because of what they had done in those two incarnations. In other words, they had to return for their *tikkun* (spiritual correction).

When we are in *galut* (exile)—and we are in galut now—we all go through pain and suffering. Whether we are in Israel or any other country, it is all the same. *Galut* is a place where there is no stability, no structure—indeed just the opposite exists. Thus out of necessity, all the souls of the tribes came down to Egypt. The Bible wants to tell us that if we do not connect to the twelve tribes of Israel, including Joseph, there is no chance of redemption. Joseph, of necessity, had to be in Egypt at this time because otherwise the Israelites would never make it out.

We have to realize that the Bible is talking about us, here and now—today. It says that all generations—past, present, and future—come down for a great purpose, which is to fulfill our *tikkun*. The Zohar says that the completion of a *tikkun* cannot be accomplished unless we connect with Joseph, and to the twelve tribes of the children of Israel. The tribes are here for us every time we are in *galut*—whether it is the *galut* of Egypt or that of Babel. Whenever *galut* takes place, the tribes are there to drag us out of it. If we do not escape *galut*, it is because we do not know how to make connections with the twelve tribes.

Significance of the Names

This section begins with the names of the sons of Jacob. Rashi points out that we have already received a precise number, as well as a precise naming of those who entered Egypt. Superficially, there seems to be very little significance to these Names. But with a greater understanding we can see the importance of these Names is that they represent the signs of the Zodiac. The stars and the cosmos exert a tremendous influence over us—an influence that, unfortunately, has been largely neglected for 4,000 years.

We read the portion of Shemot to connect with the seed level of all the Names—both those we are familiar with, and those with which we are not familiar. By virtue of the reading of the Torah Scroll, our 99 percent concealed consciousness will connect and apply the codes we refer to as "meditations" wherever there is a need for the particular combinations,

The portion of Shemot encompasses all those Names that are mentioned in the Bible. While, on a conscious level, we may be totally unfamiliar with many of the Names that exist in Kabbalah—and these are numerous, far more than we could count—we now have the good fortune to read Shemot with the assistance of the Zohar, and we can thus understand the purpose of our study. As Rav Shimon bar Yochai points out on many occasions, if we do not know why we are reading the Bible, then we have not made the connection. We are dealing with the Lightforce of God, which can enhance our lives and simultaneously remove all the chaos, pain, and suffering with which we are furnished in Creation. All that is left to humankind now is to learn how we can apply the Lightforce of God.

These Names are the channels by which we can be assured of the Lightforce of God reaching us in a manner that is individually appropriate—meaning we each receive no more than we can handle or, conversely, not so little it will not serve our purpose. The main purpose of the Names is that they are the methodology by which we can emerge from our own personal exile, which is defined by us having no control over our lives. Unfortunately, the world out there proves we are all vulnerable to events whose nature we cannot begin to imagine.

Shemot is a very significant portion because it is the Keter, the seed portion of the entire Book of Shemot. As we know, the contents and capabilities of a seed remain concealed. If we look at it, we do not see the trees, branches or fruits, yet we indubitably know it is all there in that tiny seed. So too is it with Shemot. Within this one tiny word is every conceivable combination of Hebrew letters.

The number of verses in the portion of Shemot is equivalent to the word *vayikach* ("and he will take"). What does "and he will take" have to do with this portion? When Moses divided the portions of the Torah, it was not arbitrary. Each section provides us with very specific tools by which we can be relieved of pain and suffering. The kabbalists say the time has finally come for us to take control of our destiny, rather than leave it to chance. There is only one way to succeed. To do the impossible and achieve previously unreachable goals, we have to take back (*vayikach*) "and take" what was intended at the time of Creation, and thereby gain control over our own lives.

Happiness

As we have continually stated, the Israelites never had any intention of leaving Egypt. They constantly complained to Moses about taking them away. The Bible itself says the Israelites were forced out of Egypt—and thus they always complained. They did not want to exchange the fine food they enjoyed in Egypt for life in the barren wilderness. Therefore, the Zohar states, our interpretation of this narrative is the tool and the methodology through which each of us can remove chaos from our lives.

When we say a prayer with happiness, we know that we can remove a great part of our *tikkun* process. Yet some still complain they cannot get themselves up to that level. To such people, I say, "Get you up, embrace happiness, and let us see what happens afterwards!"

If we are unhappy, the reason for such misery is simple: There is some form of chaos at the root of it. No matter the shape or color of our discontent, unhappiness cannot be represented as anything other than chaos. We cannot just tell people to be happy, though. So how do we rid the world of this kind of chaos? The methodology to remove chaos requires joy. The reason Jacob did not know that Joseph was alive—even though he was a chariot—was because of sadness. This teaches us that when we are sad or depressed we sever our contact with the Shechinah—the Creator's all-pervading feminine energy-force in our universe.

We were all present on Mount Sinai, so we could achieve immortality. The potential for immortality is right here in the universe, yet we have lost contact with it because of depression, and all the other "good" reasons we come up with to explain it.

The information contained in the seed level of Shemot is the tool we have been given to remove even the ultimate chaos—death. The Zohar constantly reminds us that to read the Bible literally is to completely miss its essential teachings.

Jacob or Israel

Shemot 1:1 says: "These are the names of the sons of *Israel* who went to Egypt with *Jacob*, each with his family." Rav Shimon asks why the Bible uses both the name Israel and the name Jacob. Either his name is *Israel* or his name is *Jacob*.

What is the purpose of the Magen David (Shield of David)? If you ask the average person, they will tell you it is simply the emblem on the Israeli flag or the sign on a synagogue. The Zohar says it is not an ornament or sign; it is a symbol of protection. It comprises two triangles, which according to Kabbalah represent the Upper and Lower Triads of the Sefirot of Zeir Anpin.

Unifying Thought and Action

From the Zohar, we know that the Sefirot of Chesed, Gevurah and Tiferet are the three Upper forces known as "Israel." The Upper Triad of the Magen David is represented as that section of the body from the breast upwards as there is a certain level of thought energy-intelligence that governs this portion of the body. The upper and lower sections of the body are separated by the diaphragm. The lower section is more evident, more active. Think about the legs. If you have a thought of walking, it cannot be manifested without feet. Of the two Triads of the Magen David, the Upper Triad is referred to as potential, and the Lower Triad as actual.

Rav Shimon explains that as the entire Book of Shemot refers to energy-intelligences, there are two aspects that must be combined: the potential and the actual. Therefore, when the Bible says *shemot benei Yisrael* "names of the sons of Israel," it is a code. We are not discussing Jacob or Israel, or the twelve tribes—we are talking about what they represent. Jacob and his twelve sons are chariots for all the forces in the universe. These twelve sons control the signs of the zodiac.

Rav Isaac Luria (the Ari), in the Writings of the Ari, explains that the souls of the generation that came to Egypt with Jacob are the reincarnation of the Generation of the Flood and the Generation of the Tower of Babel. They had still not transformed; therefore, when they came to Egypt, they did not have a connection to the Upper Realms, and were on the level of "Jacob"—a code for the Lower Triad. They did not know how to connect to the Sefirot of Chesed, Gevurah and Tiferet—the Upper Triad. In other words, the Upper and Lower Triads were separate; the head was not unified with the body, and thus thought was not unified with action. Many people act and do not think about their actions—they do not think the way they ought to think because they are not connected to themselves.

The Zohar says the reason the Bible uses two expressions—Israel and Jacob—is to tell us that these souls needed to be in Egypt. Rav Shimon says they picked Egypt over all other places because

Egypt represented the seed of all magic, sorcery, witchcraft, and all negative forces. The Israelites had to be brought there because Egypt is where the Israelites of the Flood and the Israelites of the Tower of Babel belonged—thus it was the situation from whence they all needed to elevate. The Zohar explains they descended from the heights of "Israel" and went down to "Jacob"—the Lower Triad. They were not connected to the energies of Chesed, Gevurah, and Tiferet—the Upper Sefirot. The intention was that they would, once again, learn the 72 Names of God, as well as the way these Names functioned—from the Splitting of the Red Sea to the other miracles—so that, like the twelve tribes, the Israelites would also be able to control the universe.

Satan and Chaos

As we listen to the reading of the Bible, we are taking our first steps in the removal of chaos from our lives. Within the War Rooms at our Kabbalah Centres, we are going to defeat the enemy—and this enemy is Satan. I do not have to prove this point because 3,400 years of misery and chaos are sufficient evidence to show we have travelled far enough with chaos. Finally it is time for chaos to be removed from our world. We do not have to hold on to depression, to cancer, to any form of chaos because we now have the tools to deal with it. We have the War Room, the place where the actions and the real battles take place. Our only salvation lies in a Kabbalah Centre War Room, where we can at last take advantage of the tools that the Zohar provides for our enlightenment and empowerment.

The Meaning of Exodus

We nonetheless generally refer to this section of the Bible as "Exodus," even though it has nothing to do with the exodus from Egypt. As we have heard so many times in the past, yet still must hear again, the children of Israel never had any intention of leaving that marvelous place called "Egypt." For 3,400 years, we have been told we celebrate Passover in commemoration of that wonderful event—the emancipation of the children of Israel from bondage. This is a total fabrication. The exodus from Egypt had nothing to do with the Jewish people. Why do we believe that Egypt was a country where the Israelites were physically enslaved? Clearly, the Israelites had no intention to leave and, once trudging through the wilderness, they frequently complained to Moses.

The Book of Shemot does concern an exodus—but an exodus from what? If the Bible does not mean an exodus from bondage, then what does it mean? It means the freedom to emerge from all kinds of slavery—from illness, distress, and every other form of chaos.

The Ubiquity of Uncertainty

From Kabbalah, we learn that the enemy is uncertainty. Together with chaos, uncertainty has prevailed to such an extent that in 1927 science embraced Heisenberg's Uncertainty Principle, which recognizes the ubiquity of uncertainty in all measurements of the physical universe. At the Kabbalah Centres, we boldly declare that there is also something known as certainty—and if we have certainty, there is no form of chaos we cannot ameliorate. It is incredible to find that only we kabbalists have certainty—it cannot be found anywhere else. Certainty cannot be discovered through any other means than the powerful tools provided by Kabbalah. There is no question that the forces of chaos we fight are constantly out there in our faces daily, jeering at us, not only to remind us of how uncertain this world is but also to tell us we will finally succumb to its predations. At the Kabbalah Centres, we insist there is no such thing as failure. The illusion that our efforts will not work is nothing more than an illusion.

However, my words alone cannot inspire total certainty. This can only be gained through the efforts we make with the Ana Beko'ach, and with the technology of Shabbat (the Sabbath Day). Shabbat is not solely for Jews. What about the rest of the world's people? This is a question we should have asked thousands of years ago—but we are so very timid.

The Zohar makes it extremely clear that the word "Israelite" means any people who have a direct affinity with the Lightforce of God. We have learned in Kabbalah, as expressed by the Zohar, and by Rav Isaac Luria (the Ari), that what distinguishes one person from another is their respective degrees of affinity to the Lightforce of God.

Many people actually refuse to let go of their chaos, experiencing misery day in and day out, year after year, without realizing they can put an end to it. The intent and effort to remove chaos are left to empowered individuals, a fact that demolishes the idea that we need intermediaries to help us. Humankind has never needed, and will never need, intermediaries. It is only the Lightforce of God brought to bear on any given situation that can produce the desired result—no matter how many times we have been told to give up.

The Lightforce of God

The essential character of the Lightforce of God is one of sharing. Why would we not want to share? I have heard people say they have worked so hard all of their lives, so why should they give their rewards away now? They say, "What about retirement?" It is a valid question indeed, but what they fail to recognize is that there are many things in life that cannot be bought. In fact most of the essential things in life are actually free. How much do you pay for air? What is more precious than air? What about health? We cannot purchase assurance of a complete recovery from any malady. Nor can we be assured of the total prevention of illness. The nature of the Lightforce of God consists of sharing—and not because of some moralistic principle. It has nothing to do with morality. To become like God, we have to act like God—only then are we in total control, free of all reservations. Therefore, when the Bible refers to the Israelites as the people chosen by God, it is referring to someone who is, by their nature, sharing.

Freedom from chaos depends on our consciousness and our desire to have an affinity with the Lightforce of God. When our driving force is a desire to be like God, then we truly know chaos cannot become part of our life.

With this biblical story everything is revealed. We are not discussing the children of Israel here. We are referring to those people who are, by their very nature, good people. But then there are those whose function in this world is to be evil. There are people whose purpose in life is solely one of destruction, of bringing chaos into the lives of others. Hatred for no reason begins in this portion of the Bible. The Zohar, the Talmud, and all the commentators say there was not only an exodus of Israelites but that the whole world was also enslaved by Egypt.

The Importance of Names

As we have learned in our study of Kabbalah, we cannot corrupt a word in the Bible just because it fits in with our interpretation of the text. Yet the anti-kabbalists have been successful with their corruptions to this very day because we still discuss the Book of Exodus and not the Book of Names, which is, as we know, its proper translation. As we have noted, the Hebrew word *shemot* does not mean "exodus"—it means "names." The sages and kabbalists provide a clear explanation of the meaning of "names." Names serve the purpose of enabling us to reach into the source level of things—the Keter or "Crown." This portion is the Keter, the Crown and seed of all the Names. The 72 Names of God, and the other Names revealed, are the means by which we can eliminate chaos at its root before it emerges and reveals itself. We are not here to read a story. We are here, with the help of the Zohar, to discover the importance of the Names.

The Zohar says that *Mitzrayim* (Egypt) is a metaphor for our own imprisonment. We are all imprisoned in one form of chaos or another—and most of us often find we are helpless to extricate ourselves from it. The word *Mitzrayim* implies we are locked into something, into a form of chaos. It is clearly stated in the Bible that all evil emerged from Egypt. Reflecting on this literally, it does not make sense that all evil emerged from one country, for evil cannot be a specific place in the world. The Bible is not referring to the nation of Egypt but to those aspects of negativity that create imprisonment. Such imprisonments are in the mind, and Shemot instructs us how to free ourselves from the prison in our mind.

The Book of Shemot is about practical revelation, as opposed to the potential revelation described in the Book of Beresheet. It brings us an application we must learn to use. By virtue of the Names, we have the only practical approach to removing chaos from our lives.

8 Then a new king, who did not know Joseph, came to power in Egypt. 9 "Here," he said to his people, "the Israelites have become more numerous than us. 10 Come, we must deal shrewdly with them or they will become even more numerous and, if war breaks out, will join our enemies, fight against us and leave the country."

Forgetting Joseph

From this portion, we might assume Pharaoh strategically understood that the children of Israel could wage war and then leave the country. Yet if they won this war, and succeeded in defeating Pharaoh, why would they still be obliged to leave? These verses do not make much sense literally. This new king, this Pharaoh, did not remember Joseph. After all Joseph had done for the Egyptians, how could the new Pharaoh treat the children of Israel in this manner? The Zohar makes it clear that whether or not this story happened literally, is not the Light that is being revealed in the scriptures. Pharaoh knew Joseph, and of course he remembered all that Joseph had done for him but he was afraid the Israelites would become his enemy. The new king feared for his life. So what is the connection of this to the Bible's statement that he did not know Joseph?

The Zohar explains that we cannot draw a literal idea of freedom from the words of the Bible but rather we must see that the scripture is referring to each and every one of us and our personal battle to remove ourselves from bondage—as it is manifested in our daily lives. Forget Joseph—the Bible is speaking about us today. As the Zohar says, the Bible is referring to how we develop negativity, thereby forgetting our connection to Joseph. When Pharaoh is concerned with regard to his kingdom, the Bible is actually referring to our own Satan. Pharaoh is merely a metaphor for understanding what goes on in our daily lives. The Bible is telling us that when we have a problem with conflict—in families, with our friends or in business—when we are at war anywhere, in any situation, it prevents peace from existing in our lives.

Before every important prayer, we are reminded we are not here in this physical world, we are with Joseph. Joseph is the wellspring for the energy and Light that alone can remove chaos from our lives and thus free us from bondage. We must first remember that we are constantly connected with Joseph because if we forget this we must be prepared for war, prepared to face the chaos.

The Bible is saying that when we are in the midst of facing some kind of difficult process, no matter how serious or chaotic the situation may be, if we are connected to Joseph we will know that this process will disappear. Meanwhile, we need to wash out some of the negativity we have created through our actions in this incarnation—or even in a prior one.

For more than three and a half millennia, the Bible has said the same thing. If we go the way of God, no chaos will come. But this does not seem to have worked out for us. Everyone has eventually succumbed to chaos. This is because the tools—these Names, the Ana Beko'ach—were not yet revealed. They are here now, however, but they do require the connection to Joseph—and, unfortunately, there are no connections to create this link outside the realm of Kabbalah. This is the point of the story about a relationship between Pharaoh and Joseph. There are no connections outside the realm of Kabbalah. Pharaoh (Satan in this case) rules in our lives unless we are constantly reminded of Joseph. We can make the connection to Yesod, to Joseph, in the sixth verse of the Ana Beko'ach.

More about Joseph

Joseph brought all the great wealth to Egypt—it was he who helped Egypt avert a famine that could have destroyed the whole world. The Zohar explains that this king, this Pharaoh did not remember Joseph—not because he was literally a new king but because he had a different outlook. He had forgotten about the past—all the great and good things Joseph had done—and he could only see the present now facing him.

Too often we forget the good things others do for us. The verse, "he did not know Joseph," is teaching us always to remember the good deeds people have done, and not to forget them as soon as we have a complaint. Human nature keeps us limited to seeing only what is being done for us now, and this usually leads us to forget all that was done for us in the past. From this attitude comes the expression, "What have you done for me lately?"

On Shabbat Zachor, which is the Shabbat before the holiday of Purim, we read from a section found in the Bible portion of Ki Tetze. The section reads, "Remember, remember, and do not forget." The Israelites were told three times not to forget, and yet they still forgot. We connect with this reading to help us to not only remember but also to not forget. This verse, which cautions us not to forget, indicates another aspect—one that brings *galut* (exile). Just as the "new" king forgot, the Israelites also forget—and we, too, so often forget. When we forget, we treat people only in terms of their present behavior, overlooking all the good they once did for us. In doing this, we are destined to remain in *galut*, in exile.

Who pays any attention? Even when everything around us is crumbling, we can still be in *ge'ulah* (redemption)—we do not have to be in *galut* (exile). But there are rules, and this portion exists to teach us the rules of both *galut* and *ge'ulah*. This is Redemption. It is the exodus—and this is the only way. When the rules are not followed we shall end up as the story tells us.

Rav Shimon wants to teach us some very practical things for the time we are in *galut*. The Zohar says this Pharaoh was not fit to be king because he rose to power only on account of the vast wealth behind him. Was it because of his wealth? If so, you then have to suspect wealth might not be a good thing—certainly not for the Israelites. This is a maxim we should remember because if we believe money is salvation then we have lost some valuable information.

Where do leaders come from? The Zohar says that if we think voting for someone is what made him king, we are very wrong. A king is appointed from Above. What does leadership depend on? If we are worthy of a good king, we will get a good king; if we are worthy of a bad one, we will get a bad one. The Zohar says no king, president, or prime minister is ever appointed from Below.

If we are all busy reading newspapers and watching the polls on TV, I would suggest we learn a little more Zohar instead, and not spend so much time speculating about elections. The outcomes have already been established. What does an outcome depend on? Our previous actions in many lifetimes bring leaders to the world. It is our own actions that determine what happens Above. If we do not know how to establish the ruler up there, down here it is far too late.

The Israelites controlled the vote. As Rav Isaac Luria said, concerning the Israelites in Egypt, they were souls of the Generation of the Flood and the Generation of the Tower of Babel—they were not good people, and they had not yet learned this about themselves.

This is why the portion is called Shemot. Because until this moment the people of the world did not have the Names, and thus they could not make a connection to the Lightforce of the Creator. We need to make a connection with the twelve sons of Israel, and make a connection with Joseph—because Joseph did not die. Joseph is very much here.

When we visit Joseph's grave in Nablus (Shechem, ancient Hebron), we are not going there to see the stones. We want to make a connection with Joseph the Righteous. Why do you go to visit a parent's grave—to pay your respects? This is what most people think. But to whom are you paying respect—a piece of stone, a patch of earth? We are told that, on the day a parent passes away, he or she comes back each year. They are not there all the time. Joseph is here at certain times, and he is in Hebron. We have to make the connection.

If we do not make a connection with the Lightforce of the Creator, there is no control in our life. What does control mean? The Zohar gives us all the information—everything, which is why it is called *ge'ulah* (redemption). In Rav Ashlag's commentary on the portion of Shemot, he says that if we do anything while not connected with the Lightforce of God—if we do not make these vital connections, there is no control. Then whatever can happen is going to happen. Moreover, we will be placed under the illusion we are in control, which is the most dangerous part of all.

In the section of the Zohar concerning the portion of Shemot, we see that we are not speaking of exile. Instead we are speaking of Redemption—how we can remove ourselves, elevate ourselves out of exile to achieve the level of true structure.

The "New" King and Fragmentation

There is a second interpretation in the Zohar regarding the phrase "a new king of Egypt, who did not know Joseph." But before we can understand this interpretation we first need to understand the nature of angels. Angels are the energy-intelligences that execute natural laws of the universe. An angel observes and then forms the enactment which follows a previous human activity—be it initially positive or negative—to ensure that its ultimate outcome will not be negative.

The Zohar says the entire Middle Kingdom period originated at that time because the angel who rules over all of Egypt emanated it. This is the real meaning of the phrase "a new king." As we discussed earlier, a king, leader, or president is determined in the Upper Realm. When the Bible says a new king arose, it means that at that moment, a king of destruction arose. Where does this king come from? The Zohar tells us that this kind of king originates from the place identified as "separation." As it says in the Book of Beresheet, Egypt is the first nation that created fragmentation in the world—and the reason for all chaos is fragmentation. If everyone pulled together, there would be no fragmentation. The people in the generation of the Tower of Babel were evil, and yet God could not punish them despite their negativity because they maintained a unity between themselves. When unity reigns, the natural laws of this world do not apply—even when people are thinking in a highly negative way.

With regard to the kingdom of Egypt, the angel above—the one who determines the way things are manifested—originated from the place of fragmentation. This angel was in fact the first one to be created. The reason the Egyptian king did not know Joseph, after having previously treated the Israelites so well, was because at this time, fragmentation set events in motion. The King did not know Joseph because he too was fragmentation—he was separation itself.

Joseph embodies unity—he gathers in together all the forces of the Sefirot. These are all different classifications of energy—Chesed, Gevurah, Tiferet, and so on. We make all our connections with Joseph—he is always mentioned in our prayers—because he represents unity. When it says this "new king arose," it is because he came from another place and did not know the place of Joseph—the place of unity. At this time in Egypt, the Israelites were a fragmented people—they, too, were separated from Joseph and from the unity of God.

When we think in terms of fragmentation, it really means we are separated from the Light of God. Fragmented means we are not conscious of something, and we are thus separated from it. When we are constantly aware of something, we are constantly involved with it.

11 So they put slave masters over them to oppress them with forced labor, and they built Pithom and Rameses as store cities for Pharaoh. 12 But the more they were oppressed, the more they multiplied and spread; so the Egyptians came to dread the Israelites. 13 And the Egyptians worked them ruthlessly with labor. 14 They made their lives bitter with hard labor in brick and mortar and with all kinds of work in the field; in all their hard labor they used them ruthlessly. 15 The King of Egypt said to the Hebrew midwives, one whose name was Shifrah and the second whose name was Puah, 16 saying, "When you help the Hebrew women in childbirth and observe them on the delivery stool, if it is a boy, kill him; but if it is a girl, let her live." 17 The midwives, however, feared God and did not do what the King of Egypt had told them to do; they let the boys live. 18 Then the King of Egypt called the midwives and asked them, "Why have you done this? Why have you let the boys live?" 19 The midwives answered Pharaoh, "Hebrew women are not like Egyptian women; they are vigorous and give birth before the midwives arrive." 20 So God was kind to the midwives and the people increased and became even more numerous. 21 And because the midwives feared God, He made for them houses. 22 Then Pharaoh commanded all of his people, saying: "Every boy that is born you must throw into the Nile, but let every girl live."

The Prophecy, Zeir Anpin and the Vessel

We have in this section the story of how Pharaoh realized that the *Mashiach* (Messiah) would come as a male. He instructed the midwives that whenever they assisted in the birth of a male infant they should put him to death instantly. But the midwives did not listen to this command, since they were pious, righteous women. Pharaoh summoned two Hebrew midwives to explain what had happened, and they told him Jewish women were strong, not like the women of Egypt—a child was often already born before any midwife could arrive to assist in the birth. It seems strange indeed that Pharaoh accepted this answer as the truth.

Unity and Joseph

When there is unity, there is no stronger power. If there had been unity among the Israelites, then the king of Egypt could not have created the havoc that follows—the tortures and the decrees that male children would die. The interpretations of this section state that Pharaoh's astrologers told him that an Israelite child would rise up and become the *Mashiach* who would redeem the Israelites and take them out of Egypt.

Perhaps this Israelite they referred to could have been a prophetess, like Deborah or Miriam, in which case why did Pharaoh decide to take the risk and kill only male children? Perhaps his astrologers did not see it clearly? Why would Pharaoh be kind enough to spare female children? The answer is that a man and woman complement each other. The woman is the channel by which things flourish, and the man is a channel for the life-force or the sperm. This life-force is called Zeir Anpin. Malchut is the female force, the vessel. In seeking to kill only the male children, Pharaoh was attempting to separate the six Sefirot of Zeir Anpin channeled by Joseph, putting these Sefirot to death.

In fact, the Zohar says Pharaoh was not successful because these two midwifes did not do as he instructed. The deeper implication is that when there is unity there is no place for the King of Egypt, who only represents one idea: fragmentation. Pharaoh was destined to instill fragmentation, which, even today, is the greatest tragedy befalling the Jewish people. There is this idea that we are of one persuasion, therefore we cannot get together with anyone of a different persuasion. More times than not, however, we are involved in separation.

Shemot 2:1 Now, a man of the house of Levi married a woman of the house of Levi, 2 and she became pregnant and gave birth to a son. When she saw that he was a fine child, she hid him for three months.

Hiding Moses

The Zohar says Moses was born prematurely, and that his mother was able to conceal him for three months. The people of the Middle Kingdom were of a very high level of intelligence, and could tell when a woman was pregnant. Today, a woman can take a test to determine whether or not she is pregnant, after ten days. The Egyptians could determine pregnancy without a test. They knew Yochevet had only been pregnant for six months, and so they were going to wait for three more months before they would come to claim the baby.

Why does the Bible tell us that she hid Moses for three months? The Zohar gives an entirely different interpretation. The months referred to in the Bible are the three months of the year when there is judgment, when strict rules govern us, and from which we cannot deviate—we cannot move out of these realms. It is not discussing hiding a child for three months. In these months—Tammuz, Av, Tevet—the Shechinah is concealed from us and we cannot receive its beneficence, even though God wants to give us beneficence all the time.

Through Kabbalah, and our prayers, we can connect to the Shechinah—the Shechinah being the quantum of knowledge of all things—truly knowing, not partially knowing from what can be read or may be surmised. In the three months of concealment we must be particularly aware of what we do, more so than in the other months because there is no protection afforded us by the Shechinah. This is the concealed message.

What we see on the physical level is already a manifestation. It is too late—it has happened already.

3 But when she could hide him no longer, she got a papyrus basket for him and coated it with tar and pitch. Then she placed the child in it and put it among the reeds along the bank of the Nile. 4 His sister stood at a distance to see what would happen to him. 5 Then Pharaoh's daughter went down to the Nile to bathe, and her maids were walking along the river bank. She saw the basket among the reeds and sent her slave girl to get it. 6 She opened it and saw the baby. He was crying, and she felt sorry for him. "This is one of the Hebrew babies," she said. 7 Then his sister asked Pharaoh's daughter, "Shall I go and get one of the Hebrew women to nurse the baby for you?" 8 "Yes, go," she answered. And the girl went and got the baby's mother. 9 Pharaoh's daughter said to her, "Take this baby and nurse him for me, and I will pay you." So the woman took the baby and nursed him. 10 When the child grew older, she took him to Pharaoh's daughter and he became her son. She named him Moses, saying, "I drew him out of the water."

Moses Protected

Moses' mother put him—still unnamed—in a little basket to float away on the River Nile. A miracle happened. The daughter of Pharaoh serendipitously went down into the Nile, and she saw the child. Even though she knew it was an Israelite child, she took him and raised him as her own. He was Moses, and he therefore had protection. He had to emerge safely from these waters to fulfill his destiny.

Moses—Mem Hei Shin—the Name of Healing

The importance of Shabbat Shemot is that it contains the seed of healing for the whole year—it is the origin of the 72 Names of God for healing. The name Moses (*Mem, Shin, Hei*) (מ.ש.ה) does not simply represent the name given to a baby but rather when these letters are arranged as *Mem, Hei, Shin* (מ.ה.ש) they form the most powerful name for healing known in connection with the Lightforce of God. This name is placed on the first line of the 72 Names of God chart, and we make use of it every Shabbat. There is no stronger, more effective way of tapping into the Lightforce of God—the initiator, motivator, and energizer of everything. Everything in motion in this physical world originates and is caused by the Lightforce of God. Even electricity, which is a physical energizer, has the Lightforce as its internal power.

We can engage this original power and thereby access the force of healing. This is the origin of the combination of these three letters, demonstrating the power of everything available on a physical level. Moses was a physical human being, yet he embodies something deeper, something that has greater significance than the story of a child growing up in the house of Pharaoh.

Eliminating the Irreversible

This portion is the root of the Names that can restore us. We know that healing is involved with water, and that the body is primarily composed of water—indeed the whole world is largely made up of water. Water is the root of healing. We must understand its processes, and how we can heal ourselves. At a power station, what generates the electricity? Water causes great turbines to rotate, so that they can generate electricity. It starts with water because, as I have stated here repeatedly, if anything goes wrong with the water, it can lead to only one thing—an impairment of the immune system. Everyone these days, it seems, is conducting research on the many different ways to eliminate the causes of pain and suffering. The answer is the immune system. Once we enhance, develop, and improve the immune system, no chaos can enter us again—except that we have to go through a few *tikkunim* (spiritual corrections). When we suffer a bad headache and our immune system does not take care of it, this is due to a small adjustment of our spiritual records, which has to be taken into account. We have all lived here before, and we have done negative things; therefore, a cleansing has to take place. But Moses is about eliminating something of an irreversible nature, something that creates pain and suffering.

The Tree of Life Reality

If you take the biblical story literally, Moses was doomed to be put to death by Pharaoh. He was a male child, and Pharaoh had decreed all male Israelite children should be put to death the moment they were born. Pharaoh foresaw that a male child, coming from an Israelite, would be his downfall, so it was a natural decision for him to get rid of the potential challenger and remove the problem.

The Zohar says the literal interpretation of every single word in the Bible provides us with some of the most idiotic stories we could ever dream up. Yet each and every aspect of the portion of Shemot describes this world, this universe of chaos, and at the same time informs us that there is a parallel universe known as the Tree of Life—a dimension we are all empowered to access at the time of our birth. The Tree of Life reality is not something that is beyond our capabilities to achieve. It is an allusion to the ultimate salvation.

Rav Ashlag said that in Shemot 2:10 there is an instrument to remove every form of chaos for those who have felt the need, and have the spiritual driving-force to change, to desire to be a better person—and this force is water. If one does not have this drive, then the water will not be as effective as it could be—if it is effective at all.

11 And it was in those days, after Moses had grown up, he went out to his brethren and saw their labor. He saw an Egyptian beating a Hebrew, one of his brethren. 12 Glancing this way and that and seeing no one, he killed the Egyptian and hid him in the sand. 13 The next day he went out and saw two Hebrews fighting. He asked the one in the wrong, "Why are you hitting your fellow Hebrew?" 14 The man said, "Who made you ruler and judge over us? Are you thinking of killing me as you killed the Egyptian?" Then Moses was afraid and thought, "What I did must have become known." 15 When Pharaoh heard of this, he asked that Moses be killed, but Moses fled from Pharaoh and went to live in Midian, where he sat down by a well.

The Yud, Kaf, Shin and Human Dignity

The Bible says Moses beat the Egyptian to death, and then hid him in the sand; yet the Zohar says Moses did not physically kill the Egyptian. The wisdom of the Zohar teaches us that there is no justification for doing harm to others even for all the good reasons, for all the self-validations pervading our lives, negativity will not change. The Zohar states that Moses used the 72 Names of God because he knew this methodology. He chose the *Yud, Kaf, Shin* (ש.כ.י)—the Name used for reversing the aging process. Moses merely meditated on this Name and the Egyptian died. Was Moses responsible? Yes, he was—but it was not Moses who decided this man should be put to death. Moses did not take justice into his own hands, as we often do when someone who has offended us, stolen from us or done us some other wrong.

The Bible is telling us that this man represented evil, and Moses was not the judge. The Zohar teaches that we can eliminate negativity from our midst, in any given situation, by using the *Yud, Kaf, Shin*. Moses placed in position the energies of this meditation—which is something that probably only someone like Moses could do—and in doing so, he eliminated all forms of negativity from his midst. This is the power of the Names.

What scripture wants to tell us is that when one human being does not treat another with human dignity, extreme chaos will result. The Talmud does not say the destruction of the Temple was brought about by Romans, who physically made manifest the destruction. The Talmud and the Zohar both say it was *sinat chinam*, the hatred of one Jew for another which brought about this dreadful destruction.

We are studying this portion so as to tap into the Keter, the seed level, as well as to understand that everything will emerge into knowledge, and the support-systems we need in our lives will also emerge. All the knowledge humankind requires to remove any form of chaos, including death, will not come about, even by our individual merit of connecting to the seed level, without the consciousness that we need to treat each and every single person with human dignity. If we do not treat others with human dignity, the energy and Light that Moses represents for us has to flee, has to leave our side. Moses, the one who possessed and revealed all of this knowledge, will have to depart from our individual reality, and we will not be able to avail ourselves of his direct assistance. Therefore, it is our responsibility not to validate actions of a negative nature at any time. When we validate negativity, we create an atmosphere in which Moses cannot exist. It simply does not pay. It is not beneficial for us to treat anyone with less than human dignity.

Hatred for No Reason

The Bible tells us that when Pharaoh wanted to kill Moses, Moses fled to another country and married a woman there. This shows us that conflict does not permit *Mem, Hei, Shin* (the energy of Moses) to come into being. Conflict for all of the right reasons—beating someone for all the right reasons—will boomerang back on the one who does the harm. Whether the harm is verbal or physical, we have no chance of healing ourselves or removing ourselves from chaos. It is clearly stated that Moses had to flee because of this kind of hatred.

Hatred for no reason is what prevents healing in this world. When Moses fled, it was not a physical flight. Because there was hatred for no reason, Moses had to flee. As long as it exists, people who have justified their hatred will find that, in the end, they will be the ones who suffer—they will be the recipients of their own negative actions. The Bible is clearly telling us that hatred has no place in our lives. The Talmud and the Zohar both say that the destruction of the Temple, the Holocaust, the Inquisition, and all manner of human tragedy take place for only one reason. The root cause of our own destruction is the irrational hatred of one person for another.

A foundational aspect of this portion is that hatred for no reason will not permit us to achieve freedom from our personal chaos.

Moses Killing an Aspect of Chaos

As the section continues, with extreme clarity we are told that Moses, the leader of Israel, beat another human being. The Bible is so clear in saying that he then buried him in the sand. It appears that Moses took justice into his own hands—he decided this person deserved death. Viewed superficially, this story does not make much sense. Moses, the future leader of the Israelites, is teaching us to take the law into our own hands, to kill people because we think it is right?

The Zohar says each and every single Bible story is permitting the truth to emerge. If the truth really had been so clear, the Zohar would not have come to pass. We are not learning about Moses killing an individual here. The Zohar says the word "Egyptian" in Hebrew is a code for "chaos."

The Zohar explains that, when Moses saw the Egyptian beat an Israelite, he looked this way and that—meaning he looked into the future and saw that no good would come from this man. Moses then used a Holy Name to bring Light onto the man, to remove his darkness. The Zohar says that these letters of the Ana Beko'ach— *Yud, Kaf, Shin*—are a tool we can meditate on every day, and remove chaos from our lives.

What does this story do for us today? The Zohar says stories in the Bible are all fully-coded messages, packed with extraordinary energy. When we read anything concerning Egypt in the Bible, it is not referring to the nation known as Egypt but rather it is revealing for us the tool with which we may completely emancipate the entire world.

The Harm in Hatred for No Reason

It is inferred from the words of the Bible that Moses slayed the Egyptian for all the right reasons, and from this emerges the validity of murder in the name of justice—perhaps even in the Name of God. But murder for the purpose of freedom and war in the name of humanity are never justified. So why do we keep thinking war is the tool to stop wars?

For 3,400 years, the Bible has been a part of all the monotheistic religions. Without the deeper understanding of the Bible, which the Zohar provides, we inevitably continue playing a kind of game with ourselves. The Zohar says there is no sanction for murder—there never was, and there never will be. What, then, is this story supposed to teach us?

This story provides us with a methodology of how to remove the diseases and disasters that we have, unfortunately, always blamed on God. These are the unnatural or supernatural calamities, like floods, fire, earthquakes, cancer. There is an endless list of chaos in all its forms, and humankind endures them all.

Shemot is about Names, which are combinations of Hebrew letters that the Kabbalists explain is a universal language. From the Zohar and the Writings of the Ari, we understand that Moses did not physically slay the Egyptian. The Bible itself does not say Moses committed murder. The English translation says, "...he *smote* the Egyptian and hid him in the sand." However, the Hebrew word in the biblical verse is *vayach*, which means "he beat him." So why does the translation say he "smote" or even "killed" him? Are we also to infer that Moses killed him because he buried him in the sand? What is being taught to us by the Bible is that we must eliminate chaos—and that all forms of chaos can be eliminated.

Rav Shimon explains that the Bible is referring to a three-letter combination—*Yud, Kaf, Shin*—found in the Ana Beko'ach, which Moses used to remove negativity and chaos. The *Yud, Kaf, Shin* is such a powerful instrument that we can all make use of it to eliminate the chaos that beats upon our threshold day in and day out. Rav Ashlag in the Study of the Ten Luminous Emanations teach us how to master this Name, which is difficult to fully appreciate, unless it is completely understood. We can use this three-letter combination, other Names from the Zohar, and other kabbalistic tools to be free from doubt and remove illness or pain permanently.

Keeping one's distance from chaos is a difficult chore in this world. This is why we came here—not to have a free ride but to take responsibility for our own lives and understand why we are living them. We need to ask ourselves whether we came into this world just to depart it without leaving a mark or are we going to leave this world a little better?

The Bible is not referring to the killing, beating or smiting of the Egyptian; it is referring to how Moses drew out the full dimension of chaos and buried that chaos in the sand using the Name of *Yud, Kaf, Shin*. From the Zohar we understand the significance of burying the foreskin after a circumcision. We are told the foreskin is the single entity that encapsulates the essence of chaos. If we want to remove chaos, we must return that chaos to the place from whence it came—from the earth. As we are told in Beresheet, souls do not come from the earth—a body comes from the earth. God took the earth and from it created a human body.

Where do all the problems of chaos lie, if not in the body? The soul is not affected by cancer nor is it affected by time, space, and motion. With our consciousness, we can travel anywhere in the world in seconds. The whole idea of chaos originates with the earth. The Bible tells us how we can extricate chaos from our lives through the technology of the *Mem, Hei, Shin*—and other Names we learn here.

When the two fighting Israelites turned on him, Moses discovered it was known that he killed the Egyptian. This incident is here to remind us the world was not created for the purpose of bringing chaos upon the world's inhabitants. Rather we learn from it that there is nothing more important in this world than human relationships. We learn this from the Zohar, the Ari, and all the kabbalists who have said it for millennia. It is also in fact what Hillel tried to instill and what Rabbi Akiva said as well. Hillel said, "The essential feature of the Bible is to love thy neighbor—to not do unto others what we do not want others to do unto us—the rest is commentary." We can learn all of these disciplines, and we can use all the technology of Kabbalah, but if we do not show compassion and sensitivity, even to those we have recognized as an enemy, then none of these teachings will avail us.

Satan is not in any rush. If we conduct ourselves in a negative way and instantly experience retribution, that would be too obvious— there would be no free choice or opportunity for the work involved in spiritual growth. For all the good reasons, for all the right reasons, we let our egos take over, and we forget. When we are wronged by someone, we feel we are then justified in being negative in return. Ultimately, all these justifications will come back to haunt us—and we will not escape them. One can never escape the chaos. Just look around at humankind, at all the cemeteries—how can we possibly think of immortality?

We have an opportunity with this first portion—the Keter or seed portion—of the many portions in the Book of Shemot to learn the technology to overcome chaos, to remove it at the seed level.

16 Now the priest of Midian had seven daughters, and they came to draw water and fill the troughs to water their father's flock. 17 Some shepherds came along and drove them away, but Moses got up and came to their rescue and watered their flock. 18 When the girls returned to Reuel, their father, he asked them, "Why have you returned so quickly today?" 19 They answered, "An Egyptian rescued us from the shepherds. He even drew water for us and watered the flock." 20 He asked his daughters, "And where is he? Why did you leave him? Call him so that we may break bread." 21 Moses agreed to stay with the man, who gave his daughter Tziporah to Moses in marriage. 22 Tziporah gave birth to a son, and Moses named him Gershom, saying, "I have become a stranger in a foreign land." 23 During that long period, the King of Egypt died. The Israelites moaned in their slavery and cried out, and their cry for help went up to God because of their slavery. 24 God heard their moaning and He remembered His Covenant with Abraham, with Isaac and with Jacob. 25 So God looked on the Israelites and knew about them.

Shemot 3:1 Now Moses was tending the flock of Jethro, his father-in-law, the priest of Midian, and he led the flock to the desert and came to the mountain of God in Horeb. 2 There the angel of the Lord appeared to him in flames of fire from within a bush. Moses saw that though the bush was on fire it was not consumed. 3 So Moses said, "I will go over and see this great sight—why does the bush not burn?" 4 When the Lord saw that he had gone over to look, God called to him from within the bush, "Moses! Moses!" And he said, "Here I am." 5 And He said, "Do not come any closer. Remove your sandals from your feet, for the place where you are standing is holy ground." 6 Then He said, "I am the God of your father, the God of Abraham, the God of Isaac and the God of Jacob." And Moses hid his face, because he was afraid to look at God. 7 The Lord said, "I have indeed seen the misery of my people in Egypt. I have heard their crying out from their oppressors and I know about their suffering. 8 So I have come down to rescue them from the hand of the Egyptians and to bring them up out of that land into a good and spacious land, a land of milk and honey—the home of the Canaanites, Hittites, Amorites, Perizzites, Hivites and Jebusites. 9 And now the cry of the Israelites has reached me, and I have seen the way the Egyptians are oppressing them. 10 So now, go. I am sending you to Pharaoh to bring my people, the Israelites, out of Egypt." 11 But Moses said to God, "Who am I that I should go to Pharaoh and bring the Israelites out of Egypt?" 12 And God said, "I will be with you. And this will be the sign to you that it is I who have sent you: When you have brought the people out of Egypt, you will worship God on this mountain." 13 Moses said to God, "Suppose I go to the Israelites and say to them, 'The God of your fathers has sent me to you,' and they ask me, 'What is his name?' Then what shall I tell them?" 14 God said to Moses, "I am who I am. This is what you are to say to the Israelites: 'I AM has sent me to you.'" 15 God also said to Moses, "Say to the Israelites, 'The Lord, the God of your fathers—the God of Abraham, the God of Isaac and the God of Jacob—has sent me to you.' This is My Name forever, by which I am to be remembered from generation to generation. 16 Go, assemble the elders of Israel and say to them, 'The Lord, the God of your fathers—the God of Abraham, Isaac and Jacob—appeared to me and said: I have watched over you and have seen what has been done to you in Egypt. 17 And I will bring you up out of your misery in Egypt into the land of the Canaanites, Hittites, Amorites, Perizzites, Hivites and Jebusites—a land of milk and honey.' 18 They will listen to you. Then you and the elders are to go to the King of Egypt and say to him, 'The Lord, the God of the Hebrews, has met with us. Let us take a three-day journey into the desert to offer sacrifices to the Lord, our God.' 19 But I know that the King of Egypt will not let

you go unless a mighty hand compels him. 20 So I will stretch out My Hand and strike the Egyptians with all the wonders that I will perform among them. After that, he will let you go. 21 And I will make the Egyptians favorably disposed toward this people, so that when you leave you will not go empty-handed. 22 Every woman is to ask her neighbor and any woman living in her house for articles of silver and gold, and for clothing, which you will put on your sons and daughters. And so you will take advantage of the Egyptians."

Why was Moses Chosen?

When told by God that he will be sent back to Egypt to take the Israelites out, Moses enters into a whole dialogue with God about why he is not the right person for the job. Is this the way we are meant to read this portion? I am only pointing out that nothing here can be taken literally. If we want to understand what is taking place in this section, we have to bring everything to another level of consciousness, another level of understanding.

Why was Moses chosen for this job? According to the Zohar, one explanation is that God came to this conclusion as a result of Moses' action on behalf of the lamb. If Moses could care for a little lamb too weak to walk (as a true shepherd would do), carrying it so it would not stumble alone, he surely could treat the Israelites kindly. But we should understand this explanation is not for us. There are many people today who would take care of a dog in a kindly manner. One does not have to be an evil person. If there were an injured dog in the street, many people would pick it up and try to assist the poor creature. In fact the Bible says we should address ourselves to animals that suffer. Thus Moses was no different from any other person in this respect.

If we are honest with ourselves, this is not a likely reason. So what is really happening here? There is another level of understanding. The Zohar explains that Moses was born *ki tov* (he was good). The Ari explains that Moses was born circumcised. He was born with both his *Or Penimi* (Inner Light) and his *Or Makif* (Encircling Light) present simultaneously. What does this mean? We are all born with a certain measure of Inner Light. It is what makes our body move and what allows us to think. This Inner Light also provides us with growth and gives the impetus to the DNA to do its work. The Encircling Light is the energy of fulfillment that, throughout our life, drives our desires and ambitions. Many people do not know what they want, yet from a kabbalistic point of view they are searching inwardly for their *Or Makif*—they are looking for the Light that is missing and exists outside of them. The seeker has to act to bring their *Or Makif* back to them. This task is their *tikkun* (spiritual correction).

Both Moses and Rav Shimon were born with *Or Makif*, so there was nothing more for them to do. This is why Moses was chosen. The Ari says that Rav Shimon is a reincarnation of Moses, and that Moses did not come back because he needed to make a correction (*tikkun*). He came back again for the sole purpose of reincarnating as Rav Shimon Bar Yochai.

Moses could see all the souls in existence. When Moses said "No one is going to believe me," he is in fact saying that there is another soul far greater than his own. What does "far greater" mean? Does it mean more holy? It means a vessel that can absorb a higher level of consciousness. Here Moses is referring to Rav Akiva. But God said it had to be Moses who would lead the Israelites out of Egypt.

The Midrash explains that the story of Moses' birth and concealment (for three months) is the story of Adam and Eve and the birth of their son Seth. From the birth of Cain and Abel until the birth of Seth was a span of 130 years of separation between Adam and Eve. Seth was "*tov*" (the "good" son), but, according to the Zohar, he was not completely *tov*. Amram and Yochevet were incarnations of Adam and Eve. They reincarnated for the purpose of producing Moses, a child who would be *ki tov*—he was born with both *Or Penimi* and the entire *Or Makif*.

It had to be Moses. It had to be someone who had a total connection with the cosmos—with all the knowledge of past, present, and future. Moses was chosen to lead the Israelites out of Egypt because he was born of Adam and Eve with *tikkun* (spiritual correction), and therefore he could be the channel for the Israelites. This is what Shemot is all about.

Israel is the Upper Triad and Jacob is the Lower Triad of the Magen David—there was a separation. The cosmos did not come together. The Israelites needed someone who could unite the cosmos, the Upper and Lower Triads. This man was Moses.

Woe and the Praiseworthy

Within this portion what is being spoken about is not exile but redemption—how we can remove ourselves and elevate. There is a lengthy discussion in the Zohar—in the section that deals with the portion of Shemot—that seems to have nothing to do with the portion and concerns the coming of the Messiah (*Mashiach*). This part of the Zohar says that Rav Shimon raised his hands and he wept, since this would be a time of woe (*oy*), and yet also praiseworthy (*ashrei*). The Zohar says we have always been accustomed to chaos, and this is why we find ourselves not in control. The coming of the Messiah is not referring to an "end." End, here, means that everyone will enjoy *Mashiach*, and the Zohar says we do not have to wait for such a time.

The Zohar says there will be an arousal the closer we are to the Final Redemption; and that all the nations will rise up against the Israelites. They will make decrees upon decrees, and the devastation of yesterday will be forgotten by comparison with the devastation that will follow the next day.

Yet the Zohar also says "praiseworthy" in reference to this time, declaring that it will be a merit for the person who lives at this time. Why would it be praiseworthy? We think that if we have nothing to support us then, when everything goes bad it goes bad for everyone. But the Zohar says this is not true. If we know how to make our individual connections to the Light of the Creator, even though everything around us is crumbling, it will not only be *ashrei* (praiseworthy), it will also be a merit to be there. But how can it be a merit when we see devastation around us? Are we not sensitive? Do we not feel bad that so many people are out of work, and that so many businesses are failing?

The Zohar says although everything around us will be crumbling, in the days of the coming of the *Mashiach* it will still be a merit to be there because for those who are connected they will have to ask why things are going well for them while the whole world is crumbling. Only with this question, with this awareness, will we begin to understand the power of the Lightforce of God. Without this question, when things are going well for everyone, we believe that it is we who are in control.

The Burning Bush

The Zohar refers to our time as the days of the coming of
the Messiah. Rav Shimon says those who live at this time are
praiseworthy because now, more than ever before, we have an
opportunity to see the miracle of the Burning Bush found in the
portion of Shemot.

Moses was tending the flock of his father-in-law, Yitro, and an
angel of God appeared before him in the flame of fire amidst a
bush. This is truly a miracle—everything was on fire, yet the bush
remained intact.

The Zohar explains that what Moses experienced was not a miracle
at all. It is likened to the idea that everything around us could be
burning, yet some will not feel the burning effects. The Zohar says
that in the days of the coming of Messiah those who are connected
to the Lightforce of God would have a merit and survive. Is that any
different than the bush in the midst of fire?

The Bible says Moses moved away, and that he was frightened. The
Zohar explains that God told Moses not to come closer and to
remove his shoes, for the place where he stood was Holy ground.
What does this mean? If Moses wears shoes, is it disrespectful?
Perhaps. Muslims and Hindus remove their shoes before they
pray—it shows respect for the sacred place. While removing one's
shoes in a holy environment does display respect, it also shows we
are treating this verse literally, without understanding the deeper
implications it is communicating.

The shoes God mentions here refers to the Malchut level, the closest
connection to the ground. The closest part of us to the ground is
our feet. The ground or earth means the Desire to Receive for the
Self Alone. The earth swallows up everything that comes its way.

This is its power. Not only does the earth swallow up people buried in it, the earth also has the gravitational ability to draw matter to itself.

God is telling Moses that if he wants to see miracles, he has to separate the fire from the bush, to move away from Malchut. If everything is only to be understood on a physical level, if we believe everything that is happening originates on this level, then we are lost—we can no longer be in control because we are being controlled. Despite the ramblings of our egos telling us we are in control, as long as we remain understanding things only on the level we call the physical reality, on this level of Malchut, we are not in control. The material world is actually an illusory level, since it comes and goes, it is not stationary. Nothing in the physical reality is stationary—it is the realm of ups and downs where things come and go.

The Burning Bush shows Moses there are two realities. There was fire but the bush was not consumed by it. Moses had to see the bush was not burning to know that there is a power above—the power of the Light—and thereby to understand the nature of God.

Moses was told to remove himself from the blindness of this physical world, and to connect to another level of reality where all the action is. We can also do this through prayer, with the 72 Names, with the Ana Beko'ach, and with many other kabbalistic tools. Without these tools, we are not in control, and physical reality controls us. Rav Shimon says that when Moses saw the bush remain intact without being consumed by the fire, he realized the physical laws of nature are not the laws that truly govern the whole universe—they are only in the Illusionary Realm. There are those who are connected solely with the physical reality, without an awareness of a power above—the power of God, the power of the Light. They do not know that only the Light controls.

Within God there is no murder, there are no economic problems, there are no health problems—within God these things do not exist. Because God is utterly perfect, there can be no indication of anything that originates from evil being generated within God. God has one characteristic: Sharing beneficence all the time. Therefore when something of a tragic nature occurs, we should never say that God sees this is what should happen. If something of a tragic nature happens, we have to follow what the Zohar says and separate ourselves from the Malchut—then we are not consumed on the level of the physical reality. No matter what happens around us, we can remove ourselves by making a connection with the Names and thereby with the Lightforce of God.

Negative activity and consciousness do not originate with God but with us. God follows the laws and principles of the physical universe. How can we achieve control? When we connect with the powers that be—of structure, of beneficence, of kindness, of goodness—then we are connected with the Light. In truth, only God runs this show. The only time God does not run this show is when we take ourselves out of the Realm of the Light and enter into the physical Illusionary Reality, with which God has no connection. In the physical realm God is only a producer. If a person steals then he or she has to pay for it. Did God govern the act of stealing? Stealing, as the Bible tells us, is on a physical level. Do we know why we are here? We are here to remove Bread of Shame—so why steal something? On what basis is that stolen item ours? Do we think we can get away with it?

God, as producer, puts all things together, and is always aware of every action. If misfortune occurs ten, twenty or thirty years down the road, it did not originate with God. It originates with us. The chaos that arises is the result of our negative activity and negative consciousness.

Without God, the consequences would not manifest. God follows our directives, so if we steal, then we have to pay the penalty. Yes, God, in essence, follows through with the laws and principles of the physical universe but this is only when we are involved with the physical reality.

Shemot supports us in our efforts to move away from the physical reality, so that, when there is fire, we do not get burned. God told Moses to remove the Malchut, the Desire to Receive for the Self Alone. However, the Desire to Receive for the Sake of Sharing is also a Malchut level, one that has been transformed into the level we call Zeir Anpin—a code for Joseph. By our efforts, and with the support of all of the Names, we can achieve liberation from this physical reality, even if everything around us is burning.

The Zohar, tells us we will not be affected, and more than this, we will come to realize the merit we have because we will perceive things as we never have before. If things are always good, we might think that, perhaps, the good does not come from God. We might think that maybe it is our brain, our mind, and whatever else the ego will tell us is making it so.

However, it would not be this simple if *Mashiach* came right now. Even though *Mashiach* means no more wars, no more suffering, everything peaceful, yet in the minds of many people questions would arise about what this all meant. Would we lose our possessions, the house, the car? There would be a tremendous dilemma. Wanting *Mashiach* is not such a simple thing because perhaps we do not know what it means. The burning bush teaches us that although there are laws in the physical realm, these laws can be changed.

Collective *Mashiach* means that all the physical laws will be changed. *Mashiach* for everyone can only happen when all of us achieve such an understanding. The Individual *Mashiach* is what the Bible wants to teach us about here. Before we can achieve the Collective *Mashiach*, each of us must achieve our Individual Mashiach. How do we make this arousal in the Upper Realm? How do we make this connection?

The Zohar says only with the Holy Names can we make this connection. The Holy Names have within them the ability to make this arousal. When the book of the Zohar is closed, this connection is in potential form. The moment I see the text with my eyes I have activated the Aramaic language. As the Zohar explains, the Hebrew-Aramaic language is not just a language like French, German or English, which all exist for the specific purpose of communication, and where, frequently, there are misinterpretations and miscommunications. The letters of the Hebrew language encase the Lightforce of God. The Zohar explains that we activate this Light by studying and verbalizing these letters, and even just by scanning them—for those who cannot read Hebrew. The Zohar says that just the idea of scanning the letters creates the arousal of the Light of God within those letters.

The Zohar teaches us it is only possible that this revelation will sustain the world at the time of the Messiah because of the merit possessed by Rav Shimon's generation, who were all involved in one study—the Zohar. But for now, this physical world has rules and laws, and if there is a fire, in whatever form it comes, this fire consumes everything.

What message did God want to convey to Moses when He told him to stand on his bare feet? He meant that, when we are involved with the letters and the Names, we can stand in this world and be unaffected by its ups and downs.

The Zohar says there are signs that must precede the coming of *Mashiach*—a time when the whole world has to be almost consumed by chaos. Rav Shimon and his disciples began to cry because they wondered who would be able to bear it. As long as there is chaos in the world there is no revelation of *Mashiach*, yet the Zohar adds that until the Final Redemption the letters and the *Shemot* (Names) are all going to be there. From the time of Rav Shimon until the Final Redemption, there is only the study of the Zohar, which reveals how to make the connections with the Light.

Mind Over Matter

Mind over matter is when the physical world does not control us, and we can control it. Mind over matter is a truth that has been proven by science as a physical law of the universe. However, science is theoretical. Kabbalah is practical, and on a practical level the *Shemot* (Names) create control over physical matter.

In this section, the bush was not consumed by fire, and yet we know that fire consumes everything with which it comes into contact. The Zohar says that in this section of the Bible, fire did not mean "flames." We are fortunate to be given an opportunity to reinforce our consciousness with the potentiality of mind over matter. If we do not believe in mind over matter because we are skeptical, we will be subject to the rule of this world—which is that fire consumes matter.

Today, there is no escape from airborne disease or the other ravages of physicality. We have an opportunity with this section concerning the burning bush to begin to transform our consciousness a little, to not accept that which has been there for thousands of years. Now we can begin to improve ourselves.

To Be in the Middle of Chaos and Not Be Consumed

Moses saw a bush that was on fire, yet not devoured. While everything around is burning, how can we survive? When we find ourselves in an impossible or irreversible situation, what can we do? Perhaps one has a terminal illness, and is given six months to live, and the doctors claim recovery is impossible, the disease irreversible. The Zohar says we can change all of this once and for all. We can implant into our consciousness the fact that, since human beings first roamed this Earth, chaos was not destined to remain forever. Every form of chaos that exists will ultimately be devoured, and we will leave this Earth in peace.

Shemot 4:1 Moses answered, "What if they do not believe me and listen to me and say, 'The Lord did not appear to you?'"

Believing in God, Amen

When Moses told God that he could not articulate himself, why is the first phrase in this verse, "they will not believe me," rather than, "they will not listen to my voice."?

Many people have heard me say that I do not *believe* in God, that I cannot *believe* in God. I only *know* He exists. The minute I say I do believe in God, or I do not believe there is uncertainty—belief is doubt. The moment I say I believe in God, I am saying that there is a doubt about whether or not He exists. Thus I say that I do not *believe*—I *know*. I can see the Lightforce everywhere. I can see the Lightforce in a table—not with the naked eye—but I see a dynamic dance going on in this table. Under an electron microscope, there is so much movement, so much dynamic action of atoms. The material realm does not let us see everything with the eye.

Take the word Amen, for example. The whole world says, "*Amen*"—not only Jews. For many religions *Amen* means "yes" or "I hope so." The word *Amen* (אמן) is spelled the same way as *ya'aminu* (יאמנו), which is translated as "they will believe." Here the translation of the word "believe" is a corruption because the Bible should have said the reverse, with Moses saying, "They will not listen to me, and even if they do listen to me they will still not believe me."

The numerical value of the word *Amen* is 91, and 91 is the sum of a composite of two Holy energy forces that exist in this universe: the Tetragrammaton (י.ה.ו.ה—*Yud, Hei, Vav* and *Hei*), which has the numerical value of 26, and *Adonai* (א.ד.נ.י—*Alef, Dalet, Nun* and *Yud*), another Name of God, whose numerical value is 65. The unified state of Zeir Anpin—our outer space connection, the place astronauts say is Heaven—is 91. When we bring the two worlds of Heaven above and Heaven below together (י.א.ה.ד.ה.ו.נ.ה.י), we have *Amen*. This is how we know there is unification in the world. Otherwise when we look around us at everything and everyone, all we see is separation.

Moses was in Zeir Anpin already. He was a man of flesh and bone just as we are. He was a physical human being, yet he was already *ki tov*. He could be both here now and also live in the consciousness of the dimension of Zeir Anpin—the place where, on a physical level, the astronauts say Heaven is found. All of the astronauts say they have found such great peace and tranquility in outer space that it is tangible—you could cut it with a knife. The *tzadik* (righteous soul) has such a peace and tranquility down here. Moses had it. He did not have to travel to outer space to find what astronauts only experience up there. Moses was a totality of 91.

The reason each season starts anew, when there is a completion of 91 days, is because there is a unity in the universe. However, if you look around and all you see is war and trouble, know that this is the work of humankind. Yet the sun does not fall into the Earth, the Earth does not fall into the moon; these bodies do not stray from their prescribed orbits. What holds them in place? This is still one of science's big questions. One day they will find the answer.

Kabbalists already know the answer. The unified force known as Zeir Anpin brings everything together. Zeir Anpin is a code for that place where there is pure, unadulterated completeness. This physical world is referred to as Malchut, and the Name *Alef, Dalet, Nun* and *Yud* (י.נ.ד.א) is not simply a Name, it is the manifestation of God's Lightforce in this world where things are not so complete, and where there is separation.

The energy of Egypt was of the Desire to Receive for the Self Alone. The Israelites, while in Egypt, had reached the 49th Gate of Impurity—they were almost as the Egyptians. The Israelites were under the influence of the Desire to Receive for the Self Alone, and therefore their consciousness was not in unity.

Moses, in essence, was not talking back to God. He was describing the outcome when people on different wavelengths talk about the same thing and still do not seem to hear each other because there is no meeting of the minds. Moses was saying there is Zeir Anpin and there is Malchut. When he saw that the physical bush was not consumed by the fire, he understood that Malchut could be governed by a higher consciousness. It is like fire walkers, whose feet are not burned by the hot coals. The body, which contains a human soul is, on a higher level of consciousness than the consciousness of the coal. Walking on fire is not a miracle, it is a lower-level way of comprehending the technology.

Moses saw that physicality is not what controls this world. If we want freedom, we have to recognize it does not mean that we have to leave all material wealth behind. It does not mean we have to forget about our material needs and escape to a commune somewhere—in effect to run away from society. Most people should commit to living right here, in the mud. If we think we have to run away from humanity, we have not found salvation, we have not found freedom. The only place we can find freedom is a place where physical action exists.

We want to be free of everything around us, and so we need to rule over what is around us. This is what Moses understood when he saw the burning bush. We need to make the choice, and not be governed by designer clothes, not be dictated to about what house to buy, and what car to drive. Whose standards are these? Yet such flimsy criteria are what most people live by. Thus they are not in a mental frame of unified consciousness. They are totally involved in one thing—materialism.

2 Then the Lord said to him, "What is that in your hand?" "A staff," he replied. 3 The Lord said, "Throw it on the ground." Moses threw it on the ground and it became a snake, and he ran from it. 4 Then the Lord said to him, "Reach out your hand and take it by the tail." So Moses reached out and took hold of the snake and it turned back into a staff in his hand. 5 "This," said the Lord, "is so that they may believe that the Lord, the God of their fathers—the God of Abraham, the God of Isaac and the God of Jacob—has appeared to you." 6 Then the Lord continued saying, "Put your hand on your chest." So Moses put his hand on his chest, and when he took it out, it was leprous, like snow. 7 "Now put it back on your chest," He said. So Moses put his hand back on his chest, and when he took it out, it returned to flesh. 8 "If they do not believe you or pay attention to the first miraculous sign, they may believe the latter. 9 But if they do not believe these two signs or listen to you, take some water from the Nile and pour it on the dry ground. The water you take from the river will become blood on the ground." 10 Moses said to the Lord, "Lord, I have never been an orator, neither yesterday, or the day before, nor since you have spoken to your servant. I am slow of speech and tongue." 11 The Lord said to him, "Who gave man his mouth? Who makes him deaf or mute? Who gives him sight or makes him blind? Is it not I, the Lord? 12 Now go; I will help you speak and will teach you what to

say." 13 But Moses said, "Lord, please send someone by your hand." 14 Then the Lord's anger burned against Moses and he said, "What about your brother, Aaron the Levite? I know he is well spoken. He is already on his way to meet you, and his heart will be glad when he sees you. 15 You shall speak to him and put words in his mouth; I will help both of you speak and will teach you what to do. 16 He will speak to the people for you, and it will be as if he were your mouth and as if you were God to him. 17 But take this staff in your hand so you can perform miraculous signs with it." 18 Then Moses went back to Jethro his father-in-law and said to him, "Let me go back to my brethren in Egypt to see if any of them are still alive." Jethro said, "Go in peace." 19 Now the Lord had said to Moses in Midian, "Go back to Egypt, for all the men who wanted to kill you are dead." 20 So Moses took his wife and sons, put them on a donkey and started back to Egypt. And Moses took the staff of God in his hand. 21 The Lord said to Moses, "When you return to Egypt, see that you perform before Pharaoh all the wonders I have given you the power to do. But I will harden his heart so that he will not let the people go. 22 Then say to Pharaoh, 'This is what the Lord says: Israel is my first-born son, 23 and I told you, "Let My son go, so he may worship Me." But you refused to let him go; so I will kill your firstborn son.' 24 At a lodging place on the way, the Lord met [Moses] and desired to kill him. 25 But

Tziporah took a flint knife, cut off her son's foreskin and touched [Moses'] feet with it. "Surely you are a bridegroom of blood to me," she said. 26 So the Lord let him alone. Then she said "bridegroom of blood," in regard to the circumcision.

The Significance of Brit Mila

The Zohar will provide us with a greater awareness and even an elevated consciousness to permit us to understand more fully the implications of *brit mila* (circumcision):

As a result, as long as Israel observes this covenant, the ordinances of Heaven and Earth continue to exist. But as soon as Israel do not heed to this covenant, then the covenant between the Heavens and the Earth ceases to exist, and no blessings appear in the world. Come and behold, other nations ruled over Israel only when Israel neglected this covenant. And what did they neglect? THEY PERFORMED THE CIRCUMCISION, BUT they did not uncover the corona (Heb. *pri'a*) and reveal the sacred flesh. This is why it is written, "And they forsook the Lord ..." (Shoftim 2:13) and so "He sold them to the hand of Sisra" (I Shmuel 12:9). THEREFORE, THE NATIONS DID NOT RULE OVER ISRAEL UNTIL THEY NEGLECTED THE COVENANT and they actually "forsook the Lord." This refers to what we have learned about the Holy One, blessed be He, Who said to Joshua, "Israel are not circumcised because they did not uncover the sacred flesh. Therefore they do not uphold My covenant. Yet you plan on bringing them to the land of Israel and overcoming their enemies. Circumcise again the children

of Israel a second time." (Yehoshua 5:2) And before they uncovered the corona and this covenant was revealed, they did not enter to the land of Israel and their enemies were not subdued. So here as well, when Israel volunteered to reveal the sign OF THIS COVENANT, their enemies were overcome and blessings returned to the world. Therefore it is written, "In time of tumultuous strife (also: an uncovering of flesh) in Israel, when the people willingly offered themselves, praise the Lord."
—Zohar, Lech Lecha 36: 392-394

Unfortunately there is so much ignorance surrounding the aspect of *pria*, which means the tearing of the membrane. If the membrane is not torn at the time of the *brit mila*, it is said, all of the other nations shall rule over Israel. As Elijah the Prophet said in Shoftim 2:13, "they have forsaken the Lord." When the *pria* takes place, the power of the *Yud-Hei* of the Tetragrammaton is revealed. The word pria (*Pei, Resh, Yud, Ayin, Hei*) (פריעה) is para *Yud-Hei* (פרע-יה) (*Pei, Resh, Ayin, Yud, Hei*) indicating that the Hebrew word for "tearing asunder the membrane" reveals the *Yud-Hei*.

You might say there are many other more important precepts; yet nowhere else does the Zohar make such a statement. When the *pria* occurs during circumcision, the non-Jews—those nations who are meant to put the Jews in their place—have no dominion. It does not make such a statement insofar as any other precept is concerned—only with regard to circumcision and the *pria*. And here the Zohar makes mention of another aspect of Moses when we discuss circumcision:

Another man stood up and said, as it is written, "And it came to pass on the way in the inn, that the Lord met him, and sought to kill him." (Shemot 4:24) Whom HAD HE SOUGHT TO KILL? Moses. The Holy One, blessed be

He, said to him, "You are about to go and bring Israel out of Egypt and overcome a great and powerful ruler, while you neglect a precept. Your son is not yet circumcised." Immediately then He "sought to kill him." We have learned that Gabriel came down in a flame of fire to burn him. He appeared as a burning serpent that sought to swallow him. AND HE ASKED, "Why a serpent?" AND HE REPLIED, "The Holy One, blessed be He, said to him, 'You are going to slay a great and mighty serpent, REFERRING TO THE GREAT SEA CROCODILE THAT LIES IN THE RIVERS, WHO IS THE KING OF EGYPT, while your son is not yet circumcised.'" So immediately a serpent was given the intimation to kill MOSES. However, Tziporah understood and circumcised her son, as it is written, "And Tziporah took a flint." (Heb. *tzor*) And what is a *tzor*? TZOR also MEANS a remedy. And what was the remedy? To "cut off the foreskin of her son." (Ibid. 25) So because the Holy Spirit sparkled within her, Moses was saved from death.
—Zohar, Lech Lecha 36:395-397

To find out why the eighth day is so important with regard to the circumcision, and why the drawing of blood is required, we will refer to a seemingly unrelated story that happens in Shemot 4:24, when Moses was told to go down to Egypt after he fled. He took his wife Tziporah and his two children with him: "And it came to pass on the way at the lodging place that the Lord met him and sought to kill him." The Bible says, "The Lord met him"—it does not say an Angel of Death. And it says that Tziporah took a flint and cut off the foreskin of her son and cast the foreskin at his feet. Does it mean the feet of Moses or those of the child? It does not say. But Rashi says that it was thrown at the foot of Moses; that Tziporah took a stone and cut off the foreskin, thus removing the Satan, removing the Angel of Death from Moses. And she said—I am going quote the literal expression here—"Surely a bridegroom of blood art thou to me," concerning the circumcision. This is the description of what happened, and it is quite coded.

Moses could never initiate an exodus from Egypt as long as his son was not circumcised. The purpose of the Zohar bringing in Moses at this time is to make it clear that Moses could never create a dominion over Egypt or destroy the aspect of what Egypt represented, until the *brit mila* was accomplished in his own son. When Tziporah accomplished that aspect, Moses could then go on and do what he did.

The reason Moses did not previously perform the circumcision on his son was because he knew the task that lay ahead—he was going to have to regain control and become master of the universe. The Zohar says Egypt had total control of the entire human race with their negative energy-intelligence, and that everyone fell under the influence and dominion of that Middle Kingdom. He understood that before he could create any semblance of balance in this universe he would have to confront the negative energy-intelligence, referred to as *orla*, when it became manifest. The Zohar mentions that before the Israelite can have dominion over the negative energy-intelligence called "Satan" there is another requirement necessary of the *brit mila*. If the brit mila does not cut the *orla* at its root then the root becomes manifest. Cutting something out at its root before it becomes manifest is what we are speaking about here. This is the difference between cancer that has taken hold and not permitting cancer to be in potential in the first place. Moses, like Rav Shimon (who followed in Moses' footsteps) knew that if he was now coming to attempt to take control over what I call the Dark Lord (that was Egypt), the actualization would happen when the Dark Lord is already firmly entrenched on his own turf. This is how he could take this complete embodiment of negativity at its potential and remove it by its roots. When we perform a circumcision we remove the potential but this does not mean we have now removed the dominion of Satan in the world. We have removed it for this particular individual, which is why we are required to cut Satan out right at the outset, before he can become entrenched. Moses knew what was preferable for him. He was not entering into a physical encounter with the Egyptians.

This entire encounter actually took place on the metaphysical level long before it happened. When the Israelites left Egypt, it was only an actualization of what Moses had already accomplished prior to that day. In Shemot 10:1, God said to Moses "*Bo el Paro.*" The word *bo* means "come." The Bible is saying, "Come with Me to Pharaoh." In other words, God was telling Moses to come with Him to where battle belongs—on the level of 99 Percent, on the level of consciousness where the potential, the seed lies. If we cannot create dominion over evil on a metaphysical level, then the actualization will never take place—there will never dominion of evil. Kabbalah is all about providing us with a technology and a methodology whereby we can treat the potential, the cause before the actualization.

This is the secret. While the Zohar is not always that clear, just preceding the incident with Moses, the Zohar says that the brit accomplishes dominion over the evil force. Moses needed to be in a position to take the full manifestation, not just the seed, and to eradicate it—as we do in *brit mila*. In other words, Moses took away both the potential and the actualization at the same time. To achieve this, Moses needed to deal with the actualization because when we deal only with the potential Satan is removed only from that area. *Brit mila* only removes Satan from that area. However, just because we have made *brit mila* it does not mean the Satan is eradicated from everything.

Therefore Moses permitted the kind of circumstance to arise whereby the Satan became actualized in his son, and was therefore prepared to take Moses into his clutches, and even bring him to death. This set-up was the intent of Moses. The Zohar explains that Moses needed his wife Tziporah, the Malchut, to perform the actualization. Moses performed it on the metaphysical level but the actualization of removing that *klipa* needed to be done by the Malchut. This *brit* had to be delayed so that both the potential and actualization would be eradicated.

The son was incidental because it was only Moses who performed the exodus, not the Israelites. The Israelites only displayed a little removal of their negativity because the minute they felt the slightest discomfort they wanted to go back to Egypt "where they had it good."

The Zohar says:

> Rav Aba continued, "When a man brings his son forth to elevate and initiate him to the covenant, the Holy One, blessed be He, calls upon His retinue, THE ANGELS OF HEAVEN, and declares, 'See what a creature I have made in the world.' At that time, Elijah is invited, flies over the entire world in four crossings, and then appears there." Therefore, we have learned that a man should prepare a chair in honor of Elijah, and should say, "This is the chair of Elijah." If he does not announce this, Elijah will not appear in that place nor ascend and testify about the circumcision before the Holy One, blessed be He. Come and behold, It is written first, "What are you doing here, Elijah?" (I Melachim 19:13) and "I have been very jealous for the Lord...because they have forsaken Your covenant..." (Ibid. 14) THE HOLY ONE, BLESSED BE HE, SAID TO ELIJAH, "As you live, you shall be present in every place that My sons shall imprint this Holy sign on their flesh. And the mouth that testified that Israel had

forsaken the covenant shall now testify that Israel observes it." Thus, we have learned why Elijah was punished by the Holy One, blessed be He because he accused His sons BY SAYING THAT THE CHILDREN OF ISRAEL "HAVE FORSAKEN YOUR COVENANT."
—Zohar, Lech Lecha 36:386-388

From the above passage of the Zohar, we see that Elijah is commanded, not requested by God to be present at every circumcision. It is not simply a custom that Elijah is invited to a circumcision; if he is not invited then the brit has not been completely fulfilled. This is not commonly known.

Why is it deemed a punishment for Elijah to attend every circumcision? Elijah was simply telling the truth. Should he be punished because he told the truth? What happens when he is at a *brit*? There could be hundreds of circumcisions taking place throughout the world at the same time, so how does Elijah get to all these *brits*? Why would Rav Shimon say that if we do not invite him it is almost as if the *brit* had not been completely performed? Why specifically Elijah? Jeremiah and Isaiah also criticized and reprimanded the Israelites.

From the point of view of the Zohar, it is not that Elijah is being punished; on the contrary, he comes back to this dimension in the same spacecraft that took him away. From the biblical account, it appears that Moses and Elijah both ascended into the Heavens via a spacecraft, and that these two people are very much alive and make their appearance felt on many occasions. Elijah in particular makes his presence felt at the circumcision, not as a punishment but as a double agent.

In the above Zohar we see from Rav Shimon that the entire world rests on circumcision. Rav Shimon does not mention that the balance of the world is thrown out of whack, out of balance because the Israelites worshipped idols in the past. Rav Shimon stresses the point that a particular aspect of the world's balance in the universe is predicated on the establishment of circumcision. Rav Shimon, who was an incarnation of Moses, knew the significance of *brit mila*. Rav Shimon was so powerful that he chose the day he would leave this world—the Angel of Death could not touch him. This is what we are studying here. How can we deny anyone an opportunity to access this kind of power?

The Tetragrammaton—*Yud*, *Hei*, *Vav*, and *Hei*, the intrinsic characteristic of the Lightforce—is to work in favor of positivity. However, we know *aveira* means "transgression." Does it mean the word "sin"? No. There are many other words for sin: *avon*, *pesha*, right? Now we have a new word, *aveira*, also used to indicate "transgression, sin." But *aveira* comes from that simple word, *avar*, which means "to pass over." In other words, when we create a kind of short-circuit what happens with the electricity? It is drawn into the bulb, and then where does it go? It goes into that little black space that surrounds where the electric current comes out—it has been passed over into the Dark Lord.

What happened here was, because the Satan had become manifest and actualized, he now had control of the Lightforce because he was permitted to become manifest, and he now uses that same Lightforce. As in a lightbulb, there is the positive and the negative, right? Is there a different kind of electrical current in the positive pole than there is in the negative pole? No. It is the same force—the same force that can operate in a positive way and the same force that operates in a negative way. Is there any force in this world that is not governed by the Lightforce of *Yud*, *Hei*, *Vav*, and *Hei*? Nothing happens in this Universe without the Lightforce of God. The only difference is in how this Lightforce becomes actualized. Whether, through *aveirot*, we pass it over, and it becomes manifest in the dark side or it becomes manifest in the Light side. That is the only difference. But it is always the Lightforce of God that makes things move.

The Zohar says that Satan cannot exist unless we furnish him with his sustenance. We furnish the Dark Lord with his sustenance by providing him with the energy we draw and pass over to him. When we create a short-circuit, we create something dark—and there he is, the Dark Lord. Unfortunately for most people, they can only see this situation occurring in a lightbulb. Why do you have blackened around the area where the short-circuitry occurred? Why black? Why anything? What is indicated is that the current has been passed over to the Dark Lord. And this is what happened here— thus it says that the Lightforce was being united to some extent with Satan. In fact this is the whole *tikkun* process, the spiritual correction where we draw it out.

So we understand now what Moses was out to accomplish. In other words, he was actually acting as a double agent. He was permitting the Satan to believe that he was going to become his partner—that they were going to operate together. The Lord (*Yud, Hei, Vav,* and *Hei*) and the Satan met (*vayifgeshehu*). But when they met was precisely when Moses could destroy the Dark Lord. But Moses permitted this meeting of Satan and himself to be able to provide or bring back dominion of the Lightforce over the Dark Lord (who in this case was Pharaoh).

27 The Lord said to Aaron, "Go into the desert to meet Moses." So he met Moses at the mountain of God and kissed him. 28 And Moses told Aaron everything the Lord had said, about sending him and about all the miraculous signs He had commanded him to perform. 29 Moses and Aaron went and brought together all the elders of the Israelites. 30 And Aaron told them everything the Lord had said to Moses. He also performed the signs before the people. 31 And they believed. And when they heard that the Lord was concerned about them and had seen their misery, they bowed down and worshipped. 5:1 Afterward Moses and Aaron went to Pharaoh and said, "This is what the Lord, the God of Israel, says: 'Let My people go, so that they may hold a festival to Me in the desert.'" 2 Pharaoh said, "Who is the Lord, that I should listen to his voice and let Israel go? I do not know the Lord and I will not let Israel go." 3 Then they said, "The God of the Hebrews has met with us. Now let us take a three-day journey into the desert to offer sacrifices to the Lord, our God, or he may strike us with plagues or with the sword." 4 But the King of Egypt said to them, "Moses and Aaron, why are you taking the people away from their labor? Get back to your work!" 5 Then Pharaoh said, "Look, the people of the land are now numerous, and you are stopping them from working." 6 That same day Pharaoh gave this order to the slave drivers and foremen in charge of

the people: 7 "You are no longer to supply the people with straw for making bricks like yesterday and the day before; let them go and gather their own straw. 8 But require them to make the same number of bricks as before; don't reduce the quota. They are lazy; that is why they are crying out, 'Let us go and sacrifice to our God.' 9 Make the work harder for the men so that they keep working and pay no attention to lies." 10 Then the slave drivers and the foremen went out and said to the people, "This is what Pharaoh says: 'I will not give you any more straw. 11 Go and get your own straw wherever you can find it, but your work will not be reduced at all.'" 12 So the people scattered all over Egypt to gather stubble to use for straw. 13 The slave drivers kept pressing them, saying, "Complete the work required of you for each day, just as when you had straw." 14 The Israelite foremen appointed by Pharaoh's slave drivers were beaten and were asked, "Why didn't you meet your quota of bricks yesterday or today, as before?" 15 Then the Israelite foremen went and appealed to Pharaoh: "Why have you treated your servants this way? 16 Your servants are given no straw, yet we are told to make do. Your servants are being beaten, but the fault is with your own people." 17 Pharaoh said, "Lazy, that's what you are—lazy! That is why you keep saying, 'Let us go and sacrifice to the Lord.' 18 Now get to work. You will not be given any straw, yet you must produce your full quota of bricks."

19 The Israelite foremen realized they were in trouble when they were told, "You are not to reduce the number of bricks required of you for each day." 20 They found Moses and Aaron waiting to meet them when they left Pharaoh. 21 And they said, "May the Lord look upon you and judge you! You have made us a stench to Pharaoh and his officials and have put a sword in their hand to kill us." 22 Moses returned to the Lord and said, "Lord, why have You brought trouble upon this people? Is this why You sent me? 23 Ever since I went to Pharaoh to speak in Your Name, he has brought trouble upon this people, and You have not rescued Your people at all." 6:1 Then the Lord said to Moses, "Now you will see what I will do to Pharaoh: Because of My Mighty Hand he will let them go; because of My Mighty Hand he will drive them out of his country."

Conclusion

As we mentioned previously, Rav Shimon in the Zohar of the portion of Shemot, discusses *oy* and *ashrei*—"woe" and "praiseworthy." In this section the children of Israel were complaining to Moses and Aaron about their persecution at the hands of the Egyptians. They requested of Moses and Aaron to ask for God's help. We have the tools and the awareness but unless we use them we will be persecuted—just like all the others.

Is it possible to bring down blessings by connecting to the twelve tribes? The Zohar says that connecting to the different Names is the only way we can bring blessings down from above each day—not only for ourselves but for the whole world. This is why the portion is called Shemot. As we learned, it only bears the corrupted name Exodus because the Israelites did not bring down any blessings. At some point during the many centuries since the time of the destruction of the Temple, a poisonous notion has spread regarding a "Jewish Conspiracy." It may be so—but we are not conspiring in the way anyone imagines. By our inaction, by not providing blessings to the whole world, we are guilty. So far we have not finished the job; we have not created order or brought down all of the blessings into this world.

When we pray, we must include all of the Names in Shemot. When we say *gibor* in our prayers—thinking Gevurah, "God is strong"—it is in fact only a connection to the Shemot (Names). When it says *gadol* this means Chesed. Every aspect of our prayer deals with the Sefirot, and every aspect deals with these twelve tribes. The tribes are the Names, together with Joseph. The Zohar says that the Sephardim bless their children with *Ben porat Yosef* because we must connect to Joseph, since he is the accumulation of the whole Magen David (Shield of David). Every day when we pray, we want to connect with God so that He is right here with us.

Now we understand what *shemot* means. Exodus happens by way of the *Shemot* (Names); it happens through the Names. The Zohar says that here is the beginning of the *galut* (exile) because in this Book of Shemot the Israelites went out from Egypt and because of this, some say it was their most significant action. But according to the Zohar it is not.

This entire book is teaching us how we, individually, can get out of *galut*—how we can make an exodus from our exile in chaos and disorder. We get out of *galut* through the Names. Bringing down the blessings through the Names is the only way to get out of exile.

Therefore what the portion of Shemot is dealing with is how each individual or how the whole world can come to be liberated from *galut*. According to the Zohar, the whole world is already included in the first verse. Only through the *Shemot* is there an exodus; for without the Names no exodus is possible. Only through the Names can we bring down the blessings—and only when there are blessings are we out of exile. If the whole world was filled with blessings, the Israelites would be where they have to be, and the non-Israelites would also be where they have to be—everything would be harmonious. The Zohar says that the reason this is not happening is only because we do not know how to make the connection with the Names. This connection must be made, and the secret of making it is what the portion of Shemot concerns.

BOOK OF SHEMOT:

Portion of Va'era

PORTION OF VA'ERA

Shemot 6:2 God then said to Moses, "I am the Lord. 3 I appeared to Abraham, to Isaac and to Jacob as God Almighty, but by My Name, the Lord, I did not make Myself known to them.

Certainty in the Creator is Similarity of Form with the Creator

The Zohar in the portion of Va'era begins with:

> "And God [*Elohim*] spoke to Moses and said to him, 'I am the Lord and I appeared to Abraham, to Isaac, and to Jacob, by the name of *El Shadai*....'" (Shemot 6:2-3) Rav Aba opened the discussion saying, "Trust in the Lord forever (Heb. *adei ad*), for the Lord is an everlasting rock." (Yeshayahu 26:4) "Trust in the Lord" MEANS THAT all the people of the world have to strengthen themselves in the Holy One, blessed be He, and trust in Him.
> —Zohar, Va'era 1:1

When God appeared before Abraham, Isaac, and Jacob this represented one level of the revelation of the Lightforce of God. In other words, the connection that existed between Abraham and then Jacob was on a lower level, and not the level of the Tetragrammaton—*Yud, Hei, Vav,* and *Hei.* This is the way the world is established. We will shortly come to understand the relationship between this verse of Yeshayahu (Isaiah) and the verse in the opening of the portion of Va'era.

The Zohar explains that all of humanity has to strengthen ourselves in God and be certain with Him. Does this mean that the whole world should believe in Him? How do we believe in something we have never seen? How do we understand the existence of a Higher Being—an all-powerful and all-embracing Being—when in our daily lives we do not experience the kind of unifying force that we would like to relate to God? Yet Yeshayahu 26:4 tells us this is what we have to do.

The Zohar continues:

> HE ASKS, "If so, what is the meaning of '*adei ad*'? AND ANSWERS, "It means that the strength of a person should be in the place that sustains and connects everything, and that is called '*ad*,' WHICH IS ZEIR ANPIN, as is written, 'In the morning he shall devour the prey (Heb. *ad*).' (Beresheet 49:27) '*Ad*' is the place that unites this side and that side, MEANING THAT IT IS THE CENTRAL COLUMN THAT CONNECTS THE RIGHT SIDE AND THE LEFT SIDE TO EACH OTHER, for sustenance and connecting, NAMELY, SO THAT THE TWO COLUMNS ARE SUSTAINED, AND THEIR ILLUMINATIONS ARE LINKED TO EACH OTHER,
> —Zohar, Va'era 1:2

In other words, it appears that achieving a complete and true faith in God is the purpose, and that this is what we should strive for. Of course, these are empty terms. It is like telling someone to stop smoking. There is a warning on every pack of cigarettes that tells us, "Smoking may be hazardous to your health," and yet what happens? Did everyone stop smoking? No, this warning has not influenced or convinced anyone.

The Zohar explains that to make a connection to certainty we have to first understand that there is a place known as Zeir Anpin. The Hebrew word *ad* does not mean "until." Concerning this section of the Zohar, Rav Ashlag explains that to believe in God is not a precept, it is a knowing that there is a unifying Force in this universe—the Central Column—which we understand to mean restriction. The Zohar teaches us how we can arrive at certainty. Certainty is not simply a belief in God, and thereby God will take care of everything and consequently we will no longer have any fear. We know this is not true. Look at the history of humanity and you will find that those who had complete faith in God nevertheless did not avoid the disasters that have befallen humankind for the past 2,000 years.

Says the Zohar, within each of us there are two parts: We have the Right Column and the Left Column—two aspects that are in direct conflict with each other. Should I do this? Or should I do that? Why do we have doubts? Because there are two forces operating within us: One tells us to go ahead with it, and the other tells us not to go ahead. This robotic consciousness—whether to follow this direction or that direction—was included in us at the time of our birth.

According to the Zohar, God is Zeir Anpin. What is Zeir Anpin? It is the place where everything is embraced in one unified whole. Therefore, says the Zohar, just to *believe* in the concept called certainty or to *believe* we want to become attached to certainty, cannot take place as long as there are these two conflicting forces within us. To connect with God we have to have a similitude with God. We have to have an affinity with God. How do we have an affinity with God?

Even if we desire an affinity with God, as long as there is conflict within us we are not unified with God because we are not unified within ourselves. We have not connected with God in that place where we have not been able to combine the part of us that says "no" with the part that says "yes."

Is God somewhere out there? No, God is right here. We learn in Kabbalah that every person is a part of God. Every person has God within them. What does that mean? It means succeeding in bringing together the Right Column and the Left Column, the two aspects that are in conflict within us. We achieve this through the Central Column. This is the force that synthesizes these two opposing forces; it is the Lightforce that is within the positive and the negative aspects of us. When I refer to negative or positive, I am saying *should I proceed or should I not proceed*? Yes or no? The idea that I should not proceed is a negative force. But it is not a bad force. On the contrary, this force is advising me that this would *not* be the right course of action. It is merely stating another revelation of the Lightforce of God, one that says that it would not be advantageous to follow that course.

It has nothing to do with some God out there. It has to do with the forces that God is channeled through. In a lightbulb there is a right pole and a left pole. Electricity is channeled, whether it be right or left, positive or negative; the force remains the same—electricity. So too is it with the Lightforce of God. It is channeled through a positive pole and a negative pole, through all positivity, and through all negativity. Negativity does not mean it is bad. For example, if someone who has not eaten for a few days considers the act of stealing food, and a voice from within says, "No, stealing is not something that is moral." The voice within that tells us *not* to do something is the negative voice. "Yes," on the other hand, is the positive voice telling us go ahead and *do* it (whatever it might be). Both can represent the Lightforce. The difference is how this Lightforce is expressed. The Lightforce within us is present. Unfortunately, says the Zohar, unless we are able to bring together these two opposing views, we will have uncertainty. The two opposing views within us are what creates uncertainty. However, if these two views can be brought together as one unified whole, then we can have certainty.

So it is not a question of believing in God, yet we are told, "You have to have faith in God." These are empty words. Do you think God requires that we have faith in Him when our rational mind has no conception of what that represents? Therefore the Zohar says that we are not required to believe in God—indeed we are not required to do anything. What is stated here is that there is an axiom: God is an all-embracing whole, and this Lightforce of God is within us and not out there. When we join the two opposing forces we express the Light of God. Positive expresses the Light of God and negative expresses the Light of God. However, when these two forces remain fragmented, meaning each one dominates at specific times—each one prevents the expression of the other—this is when we are uncertain. We make our connection to God when we bring together these two opposing forces.

The Zohar asks how the world maintains its stability. Of course, we have never practically seen any stability in the world but there are times that, individually, we feel fairly content—although I guess it is rare. I do not think there has been a sense of tranquility in the world since the destruction of the two Holy Temples. There are always 36 conflicts going on in the world—small ones and big ones. If the world was in harmony then the atmosphere of conflict could not exist.

How can we bring the world into a structure of balance, into a structure of tranquility? Says the Zohar, only through the Tetragrammaton—*Yud, Hei, Vav,* and *Hei*. The whole world (the unseen world and the familiar world that we see around us) was created with the first two letters, the *Yud* and the *Hei*. Both the Zohar and the Writings of the Ari explain that the *Yud* and the *Hei* are in constant unity, and that the *Vav* and final *Hei* are the problem of the Tetragrammaton.

Does this mean that Abraham was not on the level of understanding the Tetragrammaton? He was a Chariot. He had a connection to the world of the Tree of Life. Yes, Abraham was fully familiar with the existence of the Tetragrammaton. Abraham knew how to connect to the Tetragrammaton. However, until Moses came along, the Tetragrammaton was not expressed in the world. The familiar world as we see it did not experience the *Yud*, *Hei*, *Vav*, and *Hei*.

So what does the Bible mean when it says that the Name of the Tetragrammaton was not known to Abraham, Isaac, and Jacob? Says the Zohar, there were three individuals—Abraham, Isaac, and Jacob—who were familiar with this level of God's consciousness but the people, the world at large, had no idea because the Tetragrammaton was not established in the world. This level of the Tetragrammaton was not known, was not established because these three people, by and of themselves could not establish the force of unity in the world. It would have to wait until the revelation at Mount Sinai. It would have to wait until the Israelites themselves became familiar with the methodology by which they would connect with God.

How many people believe that God exists? They may say they believe in God but what does this mean? The fact that a person says they believe in God, rather than that they know God, expresses a doubt in God's existence. In the use of the word "believe" there is uncertainty. "I know" expresses the form of certainty.

The Zohar explains that when the Bible says the Name of the Tetragrammaton was not known to Abraham, Isaac, and Jacob it means that Abraham, Isaac and Jacob could not, by virtue of themselves, establish this presence in the world. How would anyone know if God is present? We might think it is when a miracle happens. But what do we mean by "miracle"? We associate good fortune with a miracle. When out of chaos comes harmony, it is often considered a miracle. And, in our vernacular, we refer to a miracle as a supernatural event, but none of these provide the correct definition. After all, is not an earthquake a supernatural event? If this definition was correct then an earthquake should be considered a miracle as well. But an earthquake is not a miracle, even though it is a supernatural event.

The Definition of a Miracle

As understood by the Bible, the definition of *nes* is not a miracle—it is a concealment. The word *nes* is comprised of two letters, *Nun* (numerical value: 50) and *Samech* (60), which together add up to 110. The Zohar says that *nes* occurs when we combine the level of Zeir Anpin, which is the Tetragrammaton—*Yud, Hei, Vav,* and *Hei* (45), and the familiar world wherein we exist, which is *Adonai*— *Alef, Dalet, Nun,* and *Yud* (65). Together they equal 110. The word *nes* in Hebrew stems from the root of the word *ve'inasu*, meaning "to run." The word *nes* itself has no association with the concept of a miracle. In fact, that is a corruption of the word.

If the word *nes* means "to run," how do we associate a miracle with running? The answer is that, aside from its concealment at the time a miracle occurs, this familiar world of chaos runs away from the world of the Tree of Knowledge. It leaves the familiar world of chaos—of *Alef, Daled, Nun,* and *Yud*—and it becomes unified with the Tetragrammaton that is spelled out in Zeir Anpin. A *nes* occurs when the world of chaos—*Alef, Daled, Nun, Yud*—takes a quantum leap into the world of Zeir Anpin. This is the idea of miracle. I will say it again: a miracle occurs when this world of physicality has elevated itself into the level of the Tree of Life—the world of certainty, tranquility, and harmony. This can only take place, says the Zohar, when the entire world recognizes and has a consciousness that there is such a world of harmony, peace, and tranquility—which is the absence of chaos. We can have control over this familiar world of chaos. This is what *Yud, Hei, Vav* and *Hei* means. When we scan the Zohar, miracles can occur.

Therefore, the Bible begins with the preface of how God appeared differently to Moses than He did to Abraham, Isaac, and Jacob. But of what concern is this to us when in essence all we are concerned about is the Israelites leaving Egypt and achieving their freedom in the world?

4 I also established My Covenant with them to give them the land of Canaan, where they lived as strangers.

Mind over Matter

Va'era is the second portion of the Book of Shemot and deals with how God appeared to Moses with a different name than He appeared to Abraham, Isaac, and Jacob. To the Patriarchs, God appeared as *El Shadai*, and to Moses He now appears as the Tetragrammaton—*Yud, Hei, Vav,* and *Hei*—which is the Lord. Why would God not use the same Name to appear to Moses as He did to Abraham, Isaac, and Jacob? Was Moses on a higher level than them? Ultimately, Moses elevated to the level of Da'at, which is above Chesed, Gevurah, and Tiferet. However, the Patriarchs were people who achieved a level that others cannot reach directly—we can only touch upon the Lower Triad (Chesed, Gevurah, and Tiferet), because the Upper Triad (Keter, Chochmah, and Binah) are on another dimension. We have the tools by which we can connect to the Upper Triad, but we cannot be a part of it.

Regarding this particular verse, even in Hebrew the Zohar is rather difficult, so in English it is almost incomprehensible. I will try to give you a general idea of what the Zohar is talking about when it refers to all aspects of the physical world—fire, water, air, and earth—that are essentially the four Sefirot, the four foundations of all physical matter. The Zohar, with Rav Ashlag's commentary (without which it would make no sense whatsoever), is very lengthy here.

In response to this first verse of Va'era, the entire aspect of physical Creation is thoroughly explained by the Zohar and Rav Ashlag's commentary in a somewhat abstruse manner. It is explained here where everything in existence comes from, the elements like gold, lead, and copper.

When we calculate the numerical value of the words *El Shadai—Alef, Lamed, Shin, Dalet* and *Yud*—they add up to 345, which is the same numerical value as *Mem, Shin, Hei*, the letters that spell Moshe (Moses). Although these letters appear in the name Moshe, Moses had this vision from God on another level. Why the differentiation? What is implied by this incredible section of the Zohar? Why do we have this section elucidating the mysteries of the physical world in this portion, when a more appropriate place for it would be in Beresheet, where it discusses the original Creation? What is more, how did Moses receive his name? His name was given to him by Batya, the daughter of Pharaoh. If Batya gave him this name, what does the Bible want to teach us? His mother Yocheved, a prophetess, and his father Amram were the parents of Aaron and Miriam, who was also a prophetess. Why did they not give Moses another name, a Hebrew name? Did the father and mother of Moses not understand that he should have a Hebrew name, and not one given by Batya?

What was the reason for the name? Was it simply because she drew him from the water? (Moshe comes from the Hebrew verb meaning "to pull out" or "draw out" of water). The answer is really very simple. We at the Kabbalah Centres say that all people are equal. Batya, who was not one of the children of Israel—although there are some commentators who say, after everything that happened in Egypt (the plagues and the freedom of the Israelites)—she too accepted the discipline of the children of Israel. The Bible wants to indicate that Moses's name did not come from an Israelite, and yet it does not make a difference.

Here the Bible makes it so clear that the name Moses—*Mem, Shin, Hei*—is a name that belongs to everyone on this planet, and we can thus merit having the God-given birthright of healing ourselves. Because the name came through Batya, it was a clear indication that everyone is entitled to heal themselves, and that this healing will come through water. In simple layman's terms, all the creatures of God around the world have the power and ability to transform something of a physical illness or ailment and to heal it.

When we raise the question of why God is introduced as *El Shadai* here, are we to understand that Abraham, Isaac, and Jacob were not aware of the new Name of God—*Yud*, *Hei*, *Vav* and *Hei*—that was given to Moses, and also that they did not know these secrets of the universe? Of course they did. In fact, Abraham was the one who revealed them in *Sefer Yetzirah* ("Book of Formation"). He was fully informed about what we can do with physical nature. This section is thus teaching us about the structure of the universe, and how it relates to the idea that the mind controls matter. On the lowest level, a layman like one of us understands that our hand, which is matter, will not respond unless there is a prior, immaterial motivation—a will to move. With this section we are going to experience the first event of control over physical reality.

Here for the first time, by the reading of this portion, we are privy not only to the idea of mind over matter but also to an actual physical demonstration of it. We are referring to the Ten Plagues, to the ten dimensions of the Satan and chaos, as well as to how we can come to ultimately control and eliminate these ten dimensions of chaos, which are known as *metzar*. As we have learnt, the word *Mitzrayim* (Egypt) is related to *metzar*, meaning a place where things are tight, a place where we feel blocked in. We are referring to the chaos that so overwhelms each and every single individual, whether it be through ailments or something else.

Therefore, the Zohar supports this endeavor of achieving control over the physical dimension of chaos. We must appreciate that from here on in, with the tools and disciplines that are being taught at the Kabbalah Centres, we can now begin to take control over the chaos that continuously gnaws at every single person.

The reason the name *El Shadai* was established here is because the Bible wants to inform us that everything existing in this physical universe is vulnerable and subject to this Name that was not mentioned before—*Yud, Hei, Vav*, and *Hei*. It is referring to the structure of the two parallel universes of Good and Evil. Where does humankind figure into this? It begins with our knowledge and the certainty that we have an ability to control matter. But the problem, I am sorry to say, is that if we have doubts this revelation from the Zohar has almost been a wasted exercise.

As we have learned, doubt is the Satan's most potent weapon. Even the financial wizards agree that financial success has to do with certainty. No businessman can ever succeed without the focus of certainty. Everyone agrees. However, there is one problem: how do you maintain certainty when chaos is staring you in the face? The Satan wants to extract that uncertainty from within us, and after this you will not ever see him—this is all he wants.

Because of scientists we have the Uncertainty Principle that all mankind must now live with. The Satan extracted this from scientists in 1927. Einstein and that whole group, with their vision of how to break down order, have caused so much misery in this world. Uncertainty still prevails to this day. Even if we have tools, once we begin to waver, everything we have learned will not be effective. If we have one doubt of uncertainty, I can tell you right now, it will fail. Without our certainty, everything we learn will not achieve for us that one objective in life: to get rid of chaos in whatever form it comes to us.

5 Moreover, I have heard the moaning of the Israelites, whom the Egyptians are enslaving, and I have remembered My Covenant. 6 "Therefore, say to the Israelites: 'I am the Lord, and I will bring you out from under the hardship of the Egyptians. I will save you from being slaves to them, and I will redeem you with an outstretched arm and with mighty acts of judgment.

Shemot 7 'I will take you as My Own People, and I will be your God. Then you will know that I am the Lord, your God, who brings you out from under the hardship of the Egyptians. 8 And I will bring you to the land I swore with uplifted hand to give to Abraham, to Isaac and to Jacob. I will give it to you as a possession. I am the Lord.'" 9 Moses spoke this to the Israelites, but they did not listen to him because of their impatience of spirit and cruel bondage.

Give Me More: Challenging the Comfort Zone

The Bible says that their cries and the pain of slavery had reached God. Yet throughout the Bible itself, as well as the Midrash and the Zohar, it is stated that the Israelites did not want to leave Egypt. Were the Israelites that senseless that the more they were beaten the more they loved it? No. Egypt represented the Desire to Receive for the Self Alone. From my study of Kabbalah I have learned to always say, "Give me more" when a challenge happens. This is because the more uncomfortable the body consciousness, the greater the spiritual growth. When we are not in "comfortability" we can get to higher levels of consciousness. But the Israelites were not learning Kabbalah at that time, since the Torah had not been given to them yet. They did not have this spiritual awareness—so they wanted to stay in Egypt.

The Israelites were not pleading to leave. In fact when Moses came to them to take them out, the Bible says the Israelites did not want to be bothered because they were too busy. Both the Zohar and the Bible say they were not interested in leaving Egypt because it was very good for them there, and what they were busy with was the material aspects. They were the same souls reincarnated from the Generation of the Flood. The Israelites were not on the level of consciousness that could take them out of bondage.

We are no different from these Israelites. We never seem to learn. Read the history of Jews in Europe. There was a decree that all the Jews had to leave and 50 or 100 years later all the Jews went back to their villages.

The time we are in now is the Age of Aquarius. It is the fourth phase of the Four Phases of Creation. And the fourth phase is Malchut. We are in Malchut, which is an appropriate time, according to the Zohar, to discuss the coming of the Messiah. The coming of the Messiah does not mean that a man on a white donkey will ride through the Gate of Mercy in Jerusalem. It does not seem logical that this is what the Bible wants to discuss.

Getting back to the original point we made, the Israelites were not on the level of consciousness that could take them out of bondage. What does this have to do with us today? For those of us who feel free, this is really unnecessary. But it is necessary for those people who do not feel gratified and do not feel the tranquility, who feel instead that something is lacking. Our trouble stems from the fact that we like to be governed by the material world, living all day in a comfortable state of mind.

The answer is that we have to be in both places at the same time. We have to know that there is a material world and also know that there is another world where we can have tranquility and peace. The universe is separated. There is the physical (*Adonai*—*Alef, Dalet, Nun* and *Yud*) and the metaphysical (Tetragrammaton—*Yud, Hei, Vav* and *Hei*). When they are brought together, this is the way we can get out of bondage, out of Egypt.

As we mentioned previously, the Hebrew word for Egypt, *Mitzrayim*, comes from the root word *metzar*, which means feeling tied up or closed in. But the Israelites did not want to get out. They were involved in the material world alone. This was the problem. There is a soul within us, says the Zohar, and that soul will always want to soar higher; it wants to go out. We will always want to feel free.

There is another important concept dealt with in the Zohar. It says that even though there may be an evil decree, if a *tzadik* says "No, not on my watch," God has to listen to him and change the decree. Does this mean that someone has to die or someone has to live, that God does not know what is supposed to happen? In other words, if someone says "No God, change your mind," does this mean that only the prophets know what tomorrow will bring, and not God?

There are many instances in the Zohar where the Angel of Death came down to destroy the world, and Rav Shimon told him to go back. The Angel of Death then came down again and Rav Shimon said, "I am here, and as long as I am here you go back and tell God that the world cannot be destroyed." Did God not know about this whole dialogue? When Moses said that the Israelites did not want to leave Egypt, God said, "You go and tell the Israelites that we are taking them out."

We learn from the Zohar that we are not to interfere with another's *tikkun* (their spiritual correction). Were the Israelites not in Egypt for *tikkun*? These same souls were here at the time of the Flood, and again at the Tower of Babel—and now in Egypt they are back again saying, "We don't want this." Both the Zohar and the Bible say that God Himself had to come and take the Israelites out of Egypt, and that without God's Force they could never get out.

In other words, if I tell someone what is good for them, what about their *tikkun*? They have to take care of their own *tikkun*. If I know what is good for them and I force them to do what I consider to be good for them, I am not permitting them to have free will to make their own choices. We learn from Rav Shimon that before we hand out free advice we have to be very careful. There is no such thing as handing out free advice without certain conditions. We just cannot say, "I know what is good for you." Everyone must have their own free will, and thus must have a choice of doing good or evil. If he or she did not have a choice of doing good or evil they would revert back to the original problem that was in the *Ein Sof* (Endless World)—which was Bread of Shame. There is a purpose to free will; and if there is a purpose and the Israelites did not want to leave Egypt, then what happened here?

To understand this further we need to go back to the Big Bang. We know that the Big Bang occurred because of Bread of Shame, which dictated free will. So the obvious question is that if God freed the Israelites from their bondage in Egypt, is this not interfering with their free will? If an Israelite decided to stay because he liked the luxury in Egypt, how can God interfere? For God has to permit free will.

Shortness of Spirit (Breath)

The exodus was not a "going out of Egypt." The Zohar says *Mitzrayim* (Egypt) means narrowness, being closed or boxed in, with no getting out. Some people find themselves in situations, whether it be in business, or in a difficult family circumstance, one from which they do not know how to get out. This is what happened in Egypt; where the Israelites were boxed in. But because they were so involved in the material world, they did not want to get out, which is why Moses had to plead with them to leave—and that if they truly wanted to have power they had to go to Israel.

Without the Lightforce of God they would have never gotten out because they were short on spirituality—*kotzer ruach*. They were working so hard that they had shortness of breath. Does this mean that they should have done some jogging and maybe then they would feel better, be trimmer and more able to work? No, *kotzer ruach* means that they were short on spirit—they did not have spirituality, and this was their trouble. When it came to the miracles, the Israelites had a short memory, and yet they could still remember the good things they had in Egypt. They did not remember the beatings; they were beaten and would come right back for more.

With regard to God, what we are speaking about is the *Or* (Light), the energy of God. In a lightbulb there are positive and negative forces; and the same force is in both, just manifested in different ways. Positive and negative energy makes the same electricity but manifest in different ways. Each of us has the same energy force but our vessel (our capacity to contain the Light) is different from one person to another.

God is only good and He puts power into this universe but because of free will, He permits us to either abuse that energy or else access the energy. The energy is for us to manipulate as we want. When the Bible says that God wanted to destroy the world, and then along came a *tzadik* (righteous person) who said no, did God then not know what tomorrow would bring? Was God not involved there?

Energy can become manifested in either way, so when a person does something, they are now on their individual track, like the track on a tape cassette. But a person has a chance to change from one cassette to another; they can jump to a parallel universe. They can get out of one spot and jump into another spot. On Shabbat, when we give new names to people, this gives the person a power to jump into another track, another cassette.

If we are not short on spirituality (*ruach*), and we are achieving a certain level of consciousness, then we can go back in time to the point where our grandfather and grandmother are still our grandparents on the old level of where we were, yet now we are on another level, we are a new person, and we can jump to a new track. We are on the level that the Israelites in Egypt were not.

Therefore, when it says that the *tzadik* could do away with a decree, he is not changing a particular cassette; the cassette itself always remains. The *tzadik* cannot change what was decreed on one path— that will always stay as it is. What he can do is jump the person from one place to another—he can assist them to change to another cassette, another track.

This is not about changing God's thoughts. God has positive and negative energy all around Him. What motivates all appliances? It is one force that becomes manifested differently. For us, this is God. He is the producer of the show and He has made many different vessels from which we can choose. Once we choose, we are on the track, and if we do not want to get off we stay there. So it is not that the *tzadik* is changing the mind of God. A *tzadik* is not necessarily a learned person—there were 24,000 learned people who could not change the decree during Rav Akiva's time. The learned scholars of Rav Akiva's day saw the destruction of the Temple. Which also brings me to the question of what the Zohar means when it says the Israelites did not want to go out of Egypt. If a person in one minute desires to be Orthodox and puts on a *yarmulke*, is he now a convert? The answer is no, he is not. All that changed is *Adonai*, the Malchut. He went from one physical expression to another. What about the *Ruach* (spirituality)? Did he change the spirit, the inside or did he simply change the clothing, the outside?

The same was so with the students of Rav Akiva. They were giants in the study of Talmud, the likes of which humanity has not seen since then. They lived during the period of the Tannaim (Rabbinic sages whose views are recorded in the Mishnah, dating from approximately 10-220 CE), and yet they could not stop the plague that killed 24,000 of them. The Zohar says that they were not *tzadikim*, they were *kotze ruach*; they did not have the spirit. Both the Zohar and the Gemarah say that a person can be learned and observant religiously, and at the same time not have *ruach*.

Having *ruach* means sharing, loving your neighbor. A person who is observant is not necessarily particular about these things but they will be aware of everything else—they will watch what they eat, how they dress, and so on. The Israelites looked different from the Egyptians but this did not make them truly different—they were still short of spirit.

Shemot teaches us how we can begin to master our own destiny; it teaches us free will—a free will that is at the same time consistent with the idea that God knows everything. Because, as we know, there are different cassettes, with different tracks. To be connected with the Bible one has to be practical—and not religious.

Rav Shimon raised his arms and cried, "Woe unto those people who will be alive in that time." "That time" means the time of the coming of Messiah—a time when the whole world will no longer be in *kotzer ruach*—no longer in bondage. Everyone will be free, and the way we can be free is when we lack for nothing. Everyone has to participate in the Age of Aquarius. This applies to all of humanity—and Rav Shimon states this very clearly.

Today, there is a revolution taking place with all of humanity, with the fundamentalists, in science, even in religion. People are no longer just leaving their faiths, they are now beginning to question whether there was ever anything there that they could truly connect with. They want to have a reason for why they should bother to connect.

How will we know the individual job has been done by all the people of the world? Is it when the word will come that the man on the white donkey has come through the gates in Jerusalem? But the Messiah is not going to do the job for us. He is not the one we should be praying for because he is only the effect of our actions. If we will do the job, he will come. It is like when you flip a switch—if you have a good lightbulb you do not have to worry if the electrical current will turn the bulb on because everyone will know if the bulb is right—the electrical current takes care of itself. It does its job. We will not be in *kotzer ruach*. Everyone will see the Messiah.

10 Then the Lord said to Moses, 11 "Come, tell Pharaoh, King of Egypt, to let the Israelites go out of his country." 12 But Moses said to the Lord, "If the Israelites will not listen to me, why would Pharaoh listen to me, since I am of uncircumcised lips?" 13 Now the Lord spoke to Moses and Aaron and commanded the Israelites, and Pharaoh, the King of Egypt, to take out the Israelites from the land of Egypt. 14 These were the heads of their families. The sons of Reuben: the firstborn son of Israel was Hanoch, and Pallu, Hezron, and Carmi. These were the families of Reuben. 15 The sons of Simeon were Jemuel, Jamin, Ohad, Jakin, Tzohar, and Saul the son of a Canaanite woman. These were the families of Simeon. 16 These were the names of the sons of Levi according to their records: Gershon, Kohath, and Merari. Levi lived 137 years. 17 The sons of Gershon, by families, were Libni and Shimei. 18 The sons of Kohath were Amram, Izhar, Hebron, and Uzziel. Kohath lived 133 years. 19 The sons of Merari were Mahli and Mushi. These were the families of Levi according to their records. 20 Amram married his father's sister Jochebed, who bore him Aaron and Moses. Amram lived 137 years. 21 The sons of Izhar were Korah, Nepheg, and Zicri. 22 The sons of Uzziel were Mishael, Elzaphan, and Sithri. 23 Aaron married Elisheba, daughter of Amminadab and sister of Nahshon, and she bore him Nadab and Abihu, Eleazar, and Itamar. 24 The sons

of Korah were Assir, Elkanah, and Abiasaph.
These were the Korahite families. 25 Eleazar
son of Aaron married one of the daughters
of Putiel, and she bore him Phinehas. These
were the heads of the Levite families. 26 It
was Aaron and Moses to whom the Lord said,
"Bring the Israelites out of Egypt by their divisions." 27 The ones who spoke to Pharaoh,
King of Egypt, about bringing the Israelites
out of Egypt were Moses and Aaron. 28 And it
was on the day that the Lord spoke to Moses
in Egypt, 29 and the Lord spoke to Moses,
saying, "I am the Lord. Tell Pharaoh, King of
Egypt, everything I tell you." 30 But Moses
said to the Lord, "Since I am of uncircumcised lips, why would Pharaoh listen to me?"

Shemot 7:1 Then the Lord said to Moses,
"See, I have made you like God to Pharaoh,
and your brother Aaron will be your prophet. 2 You are to say everything I command
you, and your brother Aaron will speak to
Pharaoh and he will send the Israelites out
of his country."

The Rational Mind Verses Consciousness

We must recognize that the Bible is not just referring to the physical
concepts that we are familiar with but also to concepts that the
rational mind cannot understand. We should place more emphasis
on consciousness, which is beyond the one percent physical
rationale we unfortunately make so much use of in our daily lives.
When we are stuck in the 1 Percent Reality, we seem to be in an

abyss of chaos. The verse begins by telling us that the level of consciousness that Moses achieved was very high, since he had true understanding. We know that there are varying levels of awareness, since two people can hear the same thing and come away with, not only different ideas but perhaps even ideas that are opposed to each other. To remove the Satan's stranglehold on our consciousness, so that we do not fall into the trap of rationale, is one of the battles we fight daily at the Kabbalah Centres.

At the beginning of the Book of Shemot, we learn to recognize what the problem is. Science does not offer this knowledge because science operates on the level of physics and physicality. The mandate of science is to study the material world, therefore it is not in its mandate to examine that which is beyond the 1 Percent Realm where the battle really takes place. We must remember that at the Kabbalah Centres we conduct services and prayer in a War Room, not a synagogue. I mean this with all my heart and in all sincerity. It is not a synagogue. We are in a war; not a war against terrorists but rather a war against that one all-embracing foe known as chaos, in whatever form it comes. Yet we continue to forget that this battle is in the metaphysical realm—the 99 Percent.

Come With Me to Pharaoh

God told Moses to come unto Pharaoh and tell him to send the Israelites out of his land. When we discuss Pharaoh and Egypt we are not referring to anything of a physical nature—not a physical individual nor a physical land. Rather we are referring to the consciousness that Pharaoh and Egypt represented. It is a metaphor. Egypt and Pharaoh symbolize chaos. This is what the Bible refers to, and it is also what the Zohar says the Bible is all about.

The children of Israel may have been slaves but not in a way we can understand slavery; they were slaves to chaos, to pain, suffering, and utter helplessness. Understanding one's own responsibility and the power to free oneself from mental and physical slavery seems like an easy task but it is exceedingly difficult to apply in a practical way. Humankind has a long history of observing itself, and yet we all return here, again and again, life after life, making the same mistakes.

How did Moses respond to God? He said, "If the children of Israel do not believe me, how will Pharaoh listen to me?" This is not referring to the Israelites in Egypt—it is a message to us about the people of today. A few verses later, in Shemot 6:30, God again told Moses to go to Pharaoh, and Moses answered, "God, don't You know I have a speech impediment?" God ignored Moses and replied, "Send Aaron." It all sounds logical enough.

Moses was not questioning God's memory now and for a second time. This passage is meant for us. When we speak to people, how many times do we repeat ourselves? "Did you not hear me the first time?" is the expression used here. Did God not hear Moses the first time? And we, the foolish people that we are, believe this is what the section is about. We are unaware of the Bible's real meaning.

We receive a strengthening of our energy when we connect with the portions of the Book of Shemot. It is so powerful for those who can raise their consciousness above the rational mind. We ought to stop for a moment and think about what we are learning at the Kabbalah Centres, and acknowledge, at least to ourselves, that although we apply what we have been taught, sometimes we do not go all the way with it—which is the main problem. As we have learned in reference to our own behavior, we must understand that we are responsible for our own chaos. We cannot blame everyone else for our problems. While there may be a perpetrator—someone or something that has inflicted pain upon us; a terrorist, a disease called cancer—until we grasp the idea that we have to take responsibility for whatever takes place in our life there is no hope of ever realizing a solution. We, you, I, all of us, will be stuck in this approach, and our life will still be chaotic.

Science has been looking for the silver bullet to destroy cancer, which destroys longevity. I will repeat what I said in the previous portion: It is the immune system that does this—period. Once again it all goes back on the individual; it is not *out there*. The reason we cannot deal with what is "out there" is because we are weak. We are so overcome by the Satan and all of his procedures that we do not have the ability to stand up. Many of us will walk away because we are weak. Maybe we are not weak not to our wives or husbands; maybe not to our children; maybe not to our employees—but essentially, we are a weakened people.

Therefore what we try to make an attempt to accomplish in the War Room, with the reading of each portion on Shabbat, is not to gather beautiful information. What we want to get is this energy so we can face up to the truth about reality and not be the wishy-washy people we have become because we are exposed to so much that overcomes and overwhelms us.

The answer is not in the silver bullet, it is in the removal of the thing that destroys our immune system, making us weak, so weak that we cannot fight back. Trees are like humans, they can experience heart attacks and even strangulation. Humans, animals, trees all experience the same things. It is the immune system that is suffering and that continues to deteriorate. With a compromised immune system there is no strength and nothing of substance or use to battle all of these diseases.

Light has that power to dispel darkness—and we are discussing the Light of God here. But we are, as Moses said about the children of Israel: "not familiar with this level of consciousness, and my words will have no meaning to them." It is beyond words; it is a Light that is not in the realm of physical reality. We cannot accomplish miracles in our life without an understanding that the 99 Percent Reality is the only aspect that will remove darkness from our lives.

Moses' Consciousness and Humility

Moses was concerned that the Israelites would not believe he communicated directly with God. Moses said that if the Israelites do not listen to him, how would Pharaoh listen? On one level, these verses teach us that we must first tackle our own problems before going after the larger issues; we must first convince ourselves of the purity of our intentions and our sincerity before taking on the world.

By his words to God Moses was revealing two things to us. One was the humility of his nature and second, Moses was saying that the Israelites were not familiar with his level of consciousness. He was implying that words would have no meaning for them, since his understanding, his consciousness was beyond words—it was a Light that is not in the realm of physical reality. We cannot accomplish miracles without an understanding that the non-rational, metaphysical part of our consciousness is the only aspect that will remove darkness from our lives.

Our Lips are the Instrument by which Our Thoughts Become Manifested

It is important to be clear about why Moses replied that he was of "uncircumcised lips," when God instructed him to speak with Pharaoh. Disregarding for a moment the various explanations given, why did he use the word "uncircumcised"? Circumcision has to do with one practice, and if the Bible meant to indicate that he had a speech impediment, why did it not say that he stuttered—why use the term "uncircumcised"?

There is an incredible lesson here from the Zohar. The Bible itself said God had to remind Moses that it was God who created him, created his mouth, and also created all of humankind. God said to Moses, "If I tell you to talk to Pharaoh, why do you not believe in Me?" Why did God not immediately give Moses the ability to speak? For both a second and a third time, God had to tell Moses to go speak to Pharaoh, and yet still God received the complaint about uncircumcised lips. It seems ridiculous. What kind of dialogue is this between a man and God?

The Zohar tells us that we are not dealing with actual lips, and we are not discussing an actual circumcision. Instead, what is being addressed is the *idea* of circumcision. The Zohar says that there are two parts to every expression. We know the power of words; sometimes we say things and we do not mean them. Every word consists of two parts: the sound, and the formation of the word. Music consists of sounds, and for that reason music is of a higher quality than words—the musical notes are on a higher level than mere words. This is why the notes do not appear in the Torah Scroll. The notes and the sounds are Zeir Anpin, says the Zohar; while the lips are the physical manifestation, the Malchut level.

The Zohar says that the contrast between the physical and spiritual dimensions is what this conversation between God and Moses concerns. When God said that Moses had to speak to Pharaoh, and Moses responded with the excuse about uncircumcised lips, Moses wished to teach us a lesson. The lips are the instrument by which our words, our voice, our thoughts become manifested and just like the foreskin, they contain the concentration of the energy of Satan.

Sometimes we can talk and talk, but what we say often falls on deaf ears. When true communication does not happen, the problem could be that it is not coming from the right place or that the words cannot be expressed properly, and thus cannot come into the level of Malchut—so the ears close and the person's receptivity shuts down.

My teacher, Rav Brandwein, used to say that some words are not meant to be understood, and that sometimes people are not meant to hear us. This dialogue between God and Moses is about the voice and words. The Israelites could not listen to Moses because he was coming from a higher level, one to which they had not yet ascended. This whole conversation between God and Moshe takes place before all the plagues are thrust on Pharaoh, which is why it had to be Aaron who would speak to him, and not Moses.

3 "But I will harden Pharaoh's heart, and though I multiply My miraculous signs and wonders in Egypt, 4 he will not listen to you. Then I will lay My hand on Egypt and I will bring out My legions, My people, the Israelites, from Egypt, with mighty acts of judgment. 5 And the Egyptians will know that I am the Lord when I stretch out My hand against Egypt and bring the Israelites out of it." 6 Moses and Aaron did so; just as the Lord commanded them they did. 7 Moses was eighty years old and Aaron eighty-three when they spoke to Pharaoh. 8 The Lord said to Moses and Aaron, 9 "When Pharaoh says to you, 'Perform a miracle,' then say to Aaron, 'Take your staff and throw it down before Pharaoh,' and it will become a serpent." 10 So Moses and Aaron went to Pharaoh and did just as the Lord commanded. Aaron threw his staff down in front of Pharaoh and his servants and it became a serpent. 11 Pharaoh then summoned wise men and sorcerers, and the Egyptian magicians also did the same things by their secret arts: 12 each one threw down his staff and they became serpents. But Aaron's staff swallowed up their staffs. 13 Yet Pharaoh's heart became hard and he would not listen to them, just as the Lord had said. 14 Then the Lord said to Moses, "Pharaoh's heart is heavy; he refuses to let the people go."

Staffs, Snakes, and Miracles

God told Moses and Aaron to create a miracle—to take a staff and throw it before Pharaoh and the staff would become a snake. A miracle is the transformation of the natural order of this world as we know it. Remember, as long as we live in this familiar world, there is only one thing we can expect: chaos. Miracles occur when we flee from the natural law and order of chaos. This is what is meant by miracle.

Chaos does not mean randomness. There is no such concept as randomness, even when chaos takes place. This has been established by science. Chaos is not the opposite of order. Chaos also follows a very particular pattern. There is law and order in chaos. When something occurs in the form of chaos, it is primarily and directly connected with an individual's action—he or she has performed, entertained, or become involved with some negative activity. The law of cause and effect exists. The result of our negativity is chaos. This is the world of *Alef, Daled, Nun,* and *Yud*—the world of Malchut; the familiar world that for us always means chaos.

But then again, who says that our familiar world must itself be comprised of chaos? This world can become connected with the same law and order of the Tetragrammaton; we can jump back and remove ourselves from this world of chaos. If at any given time in a prior or present incarnation we have become involved in some form of negative activity and now want to avoid the effect, we are told in this portion that we can convert this world. We can break into its procedures and turn them around. This is what we refer to as a miracle.

Aaron turning a staff into a snake is not the natural process of this world. In this world, a staff does not relate, nor does it have any connection to a snake. What occurred was not a disruption of this world of chaos. Rather, according to the Zohar, this world of *Alef, Daled, Nun,* and *Yud* was brought together with the world of the Tetragrammaton, the Tree of Life reality. And a staff, which is an inanimate object turned into a snake, into a living creature.

The Zohar explains the notion that a snake and a staff are two separate and distinct entities evolves only from our consciousness of the familiar world of the Tree of Knowledge. The kabbalists can look at a cube of sugar and sweeten their tea without dropping the sugar cube into it. But we cannot understand something like this because we see the eyes and the taste buds as two separate and distinct senses. We have five senses only because the world of the Tree of Knowledge, this world of *Alef, Daled, Nun,* and *Yud* appears to be fragmented. This familiar world does not seem to contain any form of law and order because in this world there is another dimension called fragmentation, which presents the illusion that things are separate from one another. The snake and the staff that we consider to be two separate entities, two separate beings, is what we refer to as the illusionary force, another ingredient that has been added to this world.

The Zohar explains that the reason the Bible begins this portion by telling us that the experience of Abraham, Isaac, and Jacob differed from that of Moses is because it is describing the combining of two worlds that both have law and order but do not have the ingredient of illusion or separation. We think we do not have the ability to look at a cube of sugar and enjoy a sweet cup of tea.

Here in this portion for the first time we have a miracle, which we can now define in terms of combining this familiar world, as we know it, with the world of the Tree of Life—meaning transforming this world of separation. For instance, when I flip a coin do I know if it will land on heads or tails? According to Kabbalah it is already known which side the coin will land on. Nothing is going to change the way this coin lies on my hand. What separates us from knowing is my other hand that covers the coin, which in kabbalistic terms is known as the curtain or veil, and it is the veil that creates illusion. The objective is to remove this illusion, which can be done. It is an illusion that only my taste buds can understand if this tea is sweet or not, and that my eye cannot tell because there are five separate senses. We have been told since we were little children that there are five senses, but this is incorrect. Each sense is combined in all the others. Every sense should be able to detect what every other sense detects, but with different levels of understanding.

What was the significance of Aaron's staff becoming a snake? Was this a miracle? No it is not a miracle. We have just been successfully programmed into believing that a snake and a staff are two separate entities, whereas in reality they are the same. One day, this curtain will be taken away and, when it will be taken away, what was always there will now make its appearance. The unity of things will appear. The unity that is the *Yud, Hei, Vav* and *Hei*—the world of the Tree of Life will make its appearance.

But for now there is a force that prevents us from experiencing this reality. The hand that covers the coin separates my vision from the reality of the coin. This is all that is involved. There is something there that prevents me from knowing if the coin is heads or tails—a curtain.

If someone recovers from an illness, is it a miracle? No, says the Zohar. The health has been there all the time, only waiting for the curtain to be removed. This individual was well even while he or she was not well. What creates the illusion and separation is the curtain. This curtain separates us from our fulfillment. If we can break through this barrier, we can have the world under control.

If someone has a family and does not have a job, it is quite obvious that they will need money to buy food. But as we have said, the money is there. So why do they not pick it up and go into the store and buy food? There is a curtain so they cannot see the money. Something conceals it. This is called the Realm of Illusion. How we have programmed our mind is the way our life will be established. We do not have to wait for it. It is like waiting until I remove my hand to know if it is heads or tails.

There is law and order in every aspect of this universe—all that is necessary is to remove the curtain. We are not creating something that is going to change the law and order because we cannot change law and order. It is like the coin; everything has already been established. When we say we do not know if it is heads or tails, we have not added that extra mile of consciousness. And because this veil can overwhelm our consciousness with separation, we really do not know.

But if we had decided, and this is what Aaron did, that the staff contains a snake, then we would know whether it was heads or tails. There is unity; the staff contains a snake and the snake contains a staff. The reason we think of snake and staff as separate is because our own consciousness is fragmented into different parts. But if we understand that everything is unified, the only thing that exists in this world is cause and effect. And even cause and effect are unified. The cause is not separated from the effect. If we can establish this truth, then we can understand clearly what is being taught here rather than just reading a wonderful story about a miracle that occurred when Aaron threw a staff on the floor and there appeared a snake.

Some of us may even understand that the apple is part of the seed and not something separate. But in our own lives do we understand the unity? Do we feel the unity? This world of illusion is giving us an opportunity to see things as separate and distinct, one from the other. But at the same time, as we learned with the word *va'era*, "he saw," he saw the curtains, and again brought together what appeared to be fragmented. Things are not separated in this world, although the curtains seem to separate things. Fragmentation exists only in our own consciousness, and if that does not exist in our consciousness, then the seed and the apple are one.

There is no such thing as "I have money today and tomorrow I will not have money." The reason we think there is no money is because our own negative activity has created a curtain. But there is no disappearance because disappearance means fragmentation. Because we have behaved in a negative way, we have created curtains and created the reality that our eyes and our taste buds are separated. With this portion we learn that separation is an illusion because there is only a curtain that does not let me see the unity of everything. The power of that curtain creates separation so that we are fully convinced the money is not there. We need to understand that chaos does not exist in this world.

The Bible is not coming to tell us a story about the greatness of Moses, about how Moses can create miracles, it is speaking about us. We are told in the portion of Va'era that humanity has the opportunity and the ability to remove our curtains. Every time we hear this portion read on Shabbat, this is the power of the removal of the curtain. Things that seem to be distant, are really not distant at all. For example, I need money but the money seems distant. I do not have it, therefore it is not there. The first consideration is to know that the money is there; however, because we do not see the money, we are not convinced the money is there, this is the problem. We cannot remove the curtain unless we remove the negative activity that created the curtain. When someone who was wealthy loses all his wealth, does this mean the money was taken away from him? No. A curtain was placed on that money to the extent that he believes the money is not there. This is how powerful the curtain is.

But Moses turned away from that illusion and did not have that consciousness. Therefore God said, "Take the staff" because it includes the snake. How do we know that the staff includes everything? What makes up 99 percent of a snake and 99 percent of a staff? Atoms. So the staff and the snake are the same. If they both have 99 percent of the same ingredients, the one percent does not make a difference. For example, if I have two cups of water, and I add one percent of cream soda in one, and one percent strawberry soda in the other, and then I add 99 percent of strawberry to both of them, they will both taste like strawberry. Everything is inclusive of everything else.

99 Percent Certainty Can Swallow up Chaos.

The Zohar says when the staff of Aaron swallowed up the staff of the Egyptian magicians this was not a magic trick. The wise men of the Egyptians were not magical entertainers. They were in a position of knowledge but they could not do what Moses could do. They could not make their staves swallow up the other staves.

There is a rule in the physical world that nothing disappears. When we see no water left, there is condensation. When the condensation disappears, there are gases. The gases go to clouds. From the clouds the water comes back again. Nothing of a physical nature disappears. This is the rule in science.

The Zohar says this consciousness is so important and that if we do not have this consciousness and understanding we cannot make it. With all the information, it is still only information. It goes in one ear and out the other. We are here for very serious business. When we enter a room and turn on the light, where does the darkness go? It is the ability of Light to remove darkness, and when we draw the Light in the chaos has to disappear. If we do not believe this to be true and still need to question what this has to do with our consciousness, then we are still stuck in the rationale of the physical. Consciousness has everything to do with physicality. This is the war we wage in our Kabbalah Centre War Rooms every day when we say *bila hamavet lanetzach* (death is swallowed up).

The most difficult thing in the world is to come to terms with the fact that there is something above the physical reality, something that consists of 99 percent, which is not physical. We are brought up, programmed, if you will, to not think in this way. Those of us who have come to this understanding about the consciousness of the 99 Percent Metaphysical Realm need to make the effort to awaken and maintain this awareness, which is what we at the Kabbalah Centres do every day. This is why we have a War Room with opportunities for tremendous spiritual connections every day. I do not miss one single day. Believe me, I would rather miss the prayer connections. I would rather not have to go through these things three or five times a day. But I know the energy and spiritual support I receive from them. We are talking about survival here.

Aaron spoke to Pharaoh and performed with the staff because Moses was on such a high level of consciousness that sometimes he could not be understood. In the same way, the kabbalists did not discuss their knowledge outright because they could not. Maybe it is easier for me because of the timing? In the mid-twentieth century, prior to the discovery of DNA, there was no way my teacher could explain to people what he understood. Science has brought us the language for all these different concepts, but science follows its own path.

Why did God tell Moses and Aaron that the staff would become a snake? In the minds of most people, a snake is one of the most fearsome creatures one can come across—its bite can be life-threatening. Moses and Aaron came to Pharaoh, threw the staff down and it became a snake. But when Pharaoh called upon his magicians to do the same, they were able to do it. Then the *etz* (staff or piece of wood) used by Aaron swallowed up the pieces of wood used by Pharaoh's magicians. The Bible uses the Hebrew word *bila*, which means "swallowed up." They were all able to transform physical matter by using the technique of mind over matter. The physical realm can be in our grasp—we can control the physical realm.

The rules of contemporary science dictate that we cannot make matter disappear—which presents a dichotomy in relation to the concept of mind over matter. How do we make things disappear? The Bible tells us staves turned into snakes and Aaron's staff swallowed up the staves of the Egyptians. What about the time in between? We are not talking about staves here; the staff is now in the form of a snake. Why not say the snake of Aaron swallowed the other snakes? What are we looking for? What does the snake represent for us? It is a teaching, and the knowledge we acquire here through Rav Shimon is to understand the message. It does not intend to tell us a story about how the snake of Aaron swallowed up the physical snakes of the Egyptians. The word for snake is *nachash*, and yet the Bible says *letaninim*, which literally translated means "crocodiles." The snake of the Egyptians represents the aspect of chaos, and we know that poison or chaos cannot eliminate other forms of chaos. Chaos will not eliminate chaos.

Is there no alternative to waging war to end injustice or applying toxic chemotherapy in the attempt to cure cancer? What else is there to use in such cases? The Bible is telling us that what is outside is not our enemy, *etz* is our answer. Swallow up our chaos;

swallow up the consciousness of the Egyptians. We are not talking about the physical Egyptians, who are wonderful people—this is a metaphor. The whole Bible, says Rav Shimon, is a metaphor. The Bible is teaching us 30th century science. Read the Zohar and this is apparent.

This section says that *etz* (wood) swallowed up the other staves because only positivity, only something that has a sharing consciousness, like a tree, can swallow up negativity. Why was *etz* used? It could have been a pipe, it could have been anything. What is the difference, a miracle is a miracle? Can a miracle not happen with anything? No, says the Zohar—and this is such a wonderful lesson—we must put in our consciousness that if we have 99 percent certainty we can swallow up chaos. We constantly work on maintaining certainty but we can lose it in a moment.

25 So they went up out of Egypt and came to their father Jacob in the land of Canaan. 26 They told him, "Joseph is still alive! In fact, he is ruler of all Egypt." Jacob was stunned; he did not believe them. 27 But when they told him everything Joseph had said to them, and when he saw the carts Joseph had sent to carry him back, the spirit of their father Jacob revived. 28 And Israel said, "I'm convinced! My son Joseph is still alive. I will go and see him before I die."

Beresheet 46:1 So Israel set out with all that was his, and when he reached Beersheba, he offered sacrifices to the God of his father Isaac.

Satan's Illusions, Consciousness, and Chaos

The Zohar asks why the staff of Aaron was used and not the staff of Moses. If you remember, the next verse says that Pharaoh called his wise people, his magicians, and they took their staves and threw them down, and they too turned into snakes. This was not a miracle only performed by Moses because the magicians of Egypt could do the same thing. These magicians also understood the principle that everything is everything, everything is like everything, and everything is a part of everything. Their consciousness dictated that since this staff contains a snake, it also contains an apple; it contains everything because it contains the 99 percent of everything else.

It is the 1 Percent Physical Reality that we refer to in Kabbalah as illusionary. Why do we refer to it as illusionary? Is the physical not a factor? Does my hand not conceal the coin? The answer is yes and no. If I decide there is no hand covering the coin, some of us would have to say there is no hand. There are times when we can look for something that is right in front of us and it is not there. This happens to us even when we do not want it to happen, even without our consciousness. We want to take a drive and we know we left the car keys on the table next to the front door but they are not there. So we run all around our home looking for the keys, only to come back to the table at the front door—and where are the keys? Right where we left them.

We did not have the consciousness to say, "Keys, you are not there." What happens that the keys can disappear even when we do not ask them to disappear? What does Satan do? He says, "Leave it alone, do not explain it because it might clarify things. Leave it alone." This is the power of what we call the illusion—this is the power of Satan.

This portion is called Va'era, which means "to see," because there are laws. We need to understand that my hand is also the coin and that it is only concealing the coin as long as my consciousness dictates. According to scientific thought, if we decide the hand is not there, it is not there. And yet science does not understand the principle that my hand and the coin are not two independent structures.

Why was the staff of Aaron used and not that of Moses? Let us start to answer this question by addressing first the distinction between the staff of Aaron and the staves of the magicians of Egypt. The Bible says that the staff of Aaron swallowed up the staff of the Egyptians. But where did Aaron's staff come from? They all turned their staves into snakes. The Bible should have said that the snakes turned back into staves and then the staff of Aaron swallowed up the staff of the Egyptians. Yet instead it says they both thrust their staves down and snakes appeared. What happened here is the clue.

The Zohar begins by asking why they did not use the staff of Moses. The Zohar answers that the staff of Moses was holier than the staff of Aaron because the staff of Moses was inscribed with the Holy Name in Upper Gan Eden (Garden of Eden). Aaron did not want the staff of Moses to come in contact with the staff of the Egyptians because if the staff of Moses swallowed up the staff of the Egyptians, it would become unholy. What is the Zohar talking about, a staff becoming holy and unholy? The Zohar tells us that the staff of Moses was at a level that he could not turn it into a snake because you can only turn something into something else in the World of Illusion. At the level of Moses, both the staff and the snake were present at the same time. There was no such thing as a staff or a snake. The 99 Percent was so evident in both that they were unified as one. With Moses' staff, there was no such thing as "it is here and it is not here" because everything is ever-present. The concept of snake and staff did not exist in the staff of Moses, so there would be no magic trick.

It is within our imagination that we see a magician make a scarf and an egg disappear. Did they really disappear? Maybe his hand is quicker than our eyes but we are all smart enough to know they did not really disappear. So then why are we so convinced? Because we do not believe it. Satan has done such a great number on us that we feel this has been embedded in our imagination. The Zohar says that the reason it appears as if nothing is there is because we know there is nothing there. If we knew there was something there it would be there.

This is what happens in the portion. The idea of a staff swallowing another staff was not a miracle at that time. The staves of the magicians of Egypt had the power of negativity—the power of illusion. The reason Aaron's staff swallowed up the magicians snakes was because Aaron was coming from another space. He was coming from the space of this world but with the ability to swallow up the illusion, and Egypt was illusion. When I say illusion, I am talking about the curtain. The Egyptians knew there was a curtain and they wanted the power of the curtain to remain. That was the power of Egypt. But along came Aaron who knew there is no such thing as a curtain, and swallowed it up because the power to remove illusion is more powerful than the power to maintain illusion. Nature is the biggest illusion. There is a force of illusion to convince us there is a force of nature but we do not know what this force is, and thus we are still looking for it. The Bible went right into the end result because it wants to tell us about the power and the ability of the removal of illusion.

15 Go to Pharaoh in the morning as he goes out to the water. Wait on the bank of the Nile to meet him, and take in your hand the staff that was changed into a serpent. 16 Then say to him, 'The Lord, the God of the Hebrews, has sent me to say to you: "Let My people go, so that they may worship Me in the desert." But until now you have not listened. 17 This is what the Lord says: By this you will know that I am the Lord: With the staff that is in my hand I will strike the water of the Nile, and it will be changed into blood. 18 And the fish in the Nile will die, and the river will stink; the Egyptians will not be able to drink its water.'" 19 The Lord said to Moses, "Tell Aaron, 'Take your staff and stretch out your hand over the waters of Egypt—over the streams and canals, over the ponds and all the reservoirs'— and they will turn to blood. Blood will be everywhere in Egypt, even in the wood and the stone." 20 Moses and Aaron did just as the Lord had commanded. He raised his staff in the presence of Pharaoh and his servants and struck the water of the Nile, and all the water in the Nile turned into blood. 21 The fish in the Nile died, and the river smelled so bad that the Egyptians could not drink its water. Blood was everywhere in Egypt.

The Plague of Blood

What difference does it make which plague came first? This revelation exists in our day; it is no longer just stories. It is not about plagues but about the reduction and the elimination of chaos. The plagues began with the Plague of Blood, which covers the dimension of Malchut, our chaotic reality of physicality. When we connect with the plagues, we will all experience not some hocus pocus story that occurred 3,400 years ago but the ability to remove chaos from our lives.

The children of Israel were the tools of Moses, and this was his unique quality. It was not that he was higher than the Patriarchs but he brought the revelation of how to remove chaos. Abraham, Isaac, and Jacob knew about it but the time had not come to reveal it in this dimension. In the dimension of time, space, and motion they were not ready. It could have been anyone but Moses was there when it was time for the revelation.

The sages said that with the first plague not only the water of Egypt but all the waters of the whole world turned into blood, and there was no water to drink with the exception of the water that was purified by the Israelites, who got paid to purify it. The Egyptians brought to the Israelites their bloody water, which they then converted to drinking water and gave back to the Egyptians.

The reason this whole world is covered with water is because without water we could not exist. Not because we would be overloaded with too much water but because water is what creates cleansing and rejuvenation. Water is the most important and most significant component of this universe.

With this idea of certainty, we can eliminate all the dimensions of negativity, so that the world can be returned to its proper place, as it was before the sin of Adam.

Controlling Water

The portion of Va'era is the physical manifestation of the power over water. With the Plague of Blood, the water was turned into blood and transformed back to water showing us that we can have control over water. The sages say that when the water turned into blood, this not only concerned Egypt but all the waters of the whole world. There was no water to drink. Like today, little by little the waters are becoming polluted; even the water we buy in bottles does not always meet FDA standards.

What does the Bible say the children of Israel did when the water turned to blood? Did they drink it? Of course they did not; one cannot drink blood and expect it to have the same effect as water. In the biblical story itself there is a lack of information, which is why we need the Zohar.

The Bible says that the children of Israel had the power to take the same bloody water and convert it into drinking water. How did they do it? Through the Zohar we see that the Israelites had the information on how to control physical matter. They had achieved a level where mind had control over matter. Only in the current age have physicists come to believe in this principle, while the kabbalists have had it for 3,400 years. All the commentators, Rashi and the Zohar included, say that this was how the Israelites became so wealthy and were able to walk out with the entire wealth of Egypt. The children of Israel had clean water, so when the Egyptians observed this phenomenon they were not concerned about the fact that they were charged exorbitant prices. Are we simply being taught about how the Israelites were such great businessmen? Before Kabbalah, this is how I understood it.

The idea of how this water was transformed never entered my mind prior to Kabbalah. The seven plagues are not to fill us with the feeling that the Israelites finally came out on top after having been the underdog for all those years. Is it supposed to give me pleasure to realize that there was a time in history when the Israelites were not scapegoats?

This section is not an opportunity to concern ourselves with the way human beings, the Egyptians or otherwise suffered, and how the children of Israel came out as heroes. We did not come here to watch a movie production so we could walk out feeling a little better. We came to tap into the power of the Bible.

The Ana Beko'ach is another tool with which we can control the physical reality. Millions of people today are using the Ana Beko'ach, and through this something is changing. However, this can only happen if we accept the idea that we want to make life a little better for ourselves. There is a tremendous difficulty in convincing people that there is a possibility to rid oneself of chaos. The truth is that science has still only uncovered three percent of what water is really all about. They do not know what water is.

Controlling Nature

The Zohar, in the portion of Va'era, devotes a great deal of time to what Rav Ashlag, with his commentary, felt it important to expand on, which is this idea of the four foundations upon which this world is built. This is the foundation of all physical matter as we know it, whether it be water, minerals, gold or silver. This section is very difficult. As I said, it took me over a year to go through about eight or nine pages of this because it is so complex. This is what the story of the plagues is all about.

Rav Ashlag gives us a commentary that we can all use, and which we can grasp by reading and scanning the Zohar. The power of the

Zohar is to provide us with clarity to receive information that our rational physical consciousness does not seem to be grasping as more than a story. This is the beauty of knowing why we want to connect with this reading. The literal stories in the Bible are just stories and, if anything, they only detract from the real point. We want to grasp the information about the secrets of the universe so that we can eliminate chaos from our lives. This is the only reason we come to Shabbat to listen to the Torah reading.

Some people are afraid of animals. Have you ever gone on a safari and petted a lion? We forget the story of Daniel in the lion's den. In the Talmud and Zohar, though not in the Bible, it says that Adam controlled all the animals. They all came over and licked his hand—the lions, tigers, even the snakes. The physical reality can be subject to man's consciousness.

By connecting to the energy afforded us through this reading we are ridding our lives of chaos. If we are still depending on 3,400 years of assurance that the Messiah is coming, we are changing the concept. Some of us are still waiting. The Messiah is not a 2,000-year-old concept—it is 3,400 years old. Of course, we could fight over who will be the Messiah—Jesus, Mohammed, or whomever—and push aside the information that the Age of Aquarius is the time when we can activate the God-like feature within ourselves that is waiting to operate for us. Do not keep it concealed. This is the most powerful time for the control of the physical reality in whatever area it is represented.

All of these plagues are not just something out of the past, they are occurring in our own time. Food is destroyed by new strains of insects—we do not even have control over a little fly. The world's food supply is being diminished every year by five percent, yet so many of us are worried about there being too many people on the planet. Why worry about the people when we should be worrying about the food and the corruption of the soil?

A little insect can destroy an entire industry, and yet we still cannot get rid of these little creatures. We have used antibiotics and pesticides for 50 years only to find out that these little creatures survive. Now the whole pharmaceutical industry has to go to a new phase of antibiotics because the old ones do not work.

While all of these apparent miracles are happening in this story, when we observe people removing chaos from their lives, why does everyone not want to jump on the bandwagon? This is because we cannot just jump on the wagon; there will not be any removal of chaos unless it is worked for and earned. The removal of chaos from our lives is up to each and every single one of us.

Converting Energy

In the portion of Va'era we have seven of the Ten Plagues, and we know that each one represents a particular Sefirot; and that these are the levels of the negative side. Each one of these plagues is truly a conversion in the same way we understand that the last plague of the Killing of the Firstborn does not mean that all the children literally died—as we will read in the next portion of Bo—it was instead a conversion of energy.

The plagues began at the level of Malchut and rose to Keter. If water is Chesed, why then is the Plague of Blood, which deals with water, the level of Malchut in this section? This is because we are discussing the Light and the Vessel, and the Vessel of Chesed comes first, while the Light comes later. Here we are dealing with the Malchut of Chesed. In Va'era we have control over seven aspects of the negative side.

Fighting the Bondage of the Desire to Receive for the Self Alone
The Plague of Blood, the Malchut, is the first of ten miracles that
were channeled by Moses and Aaron to the ten levels of chaos. This
was not chaos on a physical level; the war with chaos does not
take place on a physical level. Science has more than witnessed
this throughout the ages. Today, the world has been able to
create miracles.

Concerning chaos, are the physical terrorists the problem? If we get
rid of them, meaning the physical person, will we remove terrorism?
No, because on the other level, the immaterial level, the terrorists
will still be there. We cannot remove chaos by any physical means—
never. The physical instrument is not where the action takes place.

Therefore, the first miracle was water; all the waters of the world,
not only of Egypt turned into blood. Even here the commentators
joked that the children of Israel could take water and turn it into
blood, and then turn it back into water and sell it to the Egyptians.
Is this supposed to teach us about Israelites? Both the Bible and the
Zohar say this is not the lesson. It is not about having a Passover
dinner and celebrating the death of the Egyptians. This is not
about the Egyptians or the Israelites; we are fighting the metaphor
that represents chaos. The Egyptians represented the chaos of this
physical world, which is a bondage to the Desire to Receive for the
Self Alone.

There was a miracle where they transformed the blood back into
water. When Pharaoh pleaded that he would let the children of
Israel go, what happened to the blood? The power of positivity
swallowed up the negativity. Does it matter where it went? If
we need light and the electrical system is out, do we care about
anything other than getting the lights on? With the portion
of Va'era we remove chaos at its metaphysical level, going from
Malchut to Chesed, with the first seven Plagues, which are

essentially not plagues but metaphors for chaos and their conversion into miracles.

In the portion of Bo, we will finish off the totality of the metaphysical power of the Satan—the final three negative levels of energy. But remember, if we are fighting it on a physical level, we cannot remove chaos.

22 But the Egyptian magicians did the same things by their secret arts, and Pharaoh's heart became hard; he would not listen to Moses and Aaron, just as the Lord had said. 23 Instead, he turned and went into his palace, and did not take even this to heart. 24 And all the Egyptians dug along the Nile to get drinking water, because they could not drink the water of the river. 25 Seven days passed after the Lord struck the Nile. 26 Then the Lord said to Moses, "Come to Pharaoh and say to him, 'This is what the Lord says: "Let My people go, so that they may worship Me." 27 If you refuse to let them go, I will plague your whole country with frogs. 28 The Nile will teem with frogs. They will come up into your palace and your bedroom and onto your bed, into the houses of your servants and on your people, and into your ovens and kneading troughs. 29 The frogs will go up on you and your people and all your servants.'"

Shemot 8:1 Then the Lord said to Moses, "Tell Aaron, 'Stretch out your hand with your staff over the streams and canals and ponds, and make frogs come up on the land of Egypt.'" 2 So Aaron stretched out his hand over the waters of Egypt, and the frogs came up and covered the land of Egypt. 3 But the magicians did the same things by their secret arts; they also made frogs come up on the land of Egypt. 4 Pharaoh summoned Moses and Aaron and said, "Pray to the Lord to take the frogs away from me and my people, and I will let your people go and offer sacrifices to the Lord." 5 Moses said to Pharaoh, "I leave to you the honor of setting the time for me to pray for you and your officials and your people that you and your houses may be rid of the frogs, except for those that remain in the Nile." 6 "Tomorrow," Pharaoh said. Moses replied, "It will be as you say, so that you may know there is no one like the Lord, our God. 7 The frogs will leave you and your houses, your servants and your people; they will remain only in the Nile." 8 After Moses and Aaron left Pharaoh, Moses cried out to the Lord about the frogs he had brought on Pharaoh. 9 And the Lord did what Moses asked. The frogs died in the houses, in the courtyards and in the fields. 10 They were piled into heaps, and the land reeked of them. 11 But when Pharaoh saw that there was relief, he hardened his heart and would not listen to them, just as the Lord had said. 12 Then the Lord said to Moses, "Tell Aaron, 'Stretch out your staff and strike the dust of the ground,' and throughout the land of Egypt it will become lice." 13 They did this, and when Aaron stretched out his hand with the staff and struck the dust of the ground, lice came upon men and animals. All the dust throughout the land of Egypt became lice. 14 But when the magicians tried to produce lice by their secret arts, they could not. And the lice were on men and animals. 15 The magicians said to Pharaoh, "This is the Finger of God." But Pharaoh's heart was hard and he would not listen to them, just as the Lord had said. 16 The Lord said to Moses, "Get up early in the morning and confront Pharaoh as he goes to the water and say to him, 'This is what the Lord says: "Let My people go, so that they may worship Me." 17 If you do not let My people go, I will send wild animals on you and your servants, on your people and into your houses. The houses of the Egyptians will be full of wild animals, and even the ground where they are. 18 But on that day I will deal differently with the land of Goshen, where My people live; no wild animals will be there, so that you will know that I, the Lord, am in this land. 19 I will make a distinction between My people and your people. This miraculous sign will occur tomorrow.'" 20 And the Lord did this, and a heavy swarm of wild animals poured into Pharaoh's palace and into the houses of his servants, and throughout Egypt the land was ruined by the wild animals. 21 Then Pharaoh summoned Moses and Aaron and said, "Go, sacrifice to your God here in the land." 22 But Moses said, "That would not be right. The sacrifices we offer the Lord, our God, would be detestable to the Egyptians. And if we offer sacrifices that are detestable in their eyes, will they not stone us? 23 We must take a three-day journey into the desert and offer sacrifices to the Lord, our God, as He tells us." 24 Pharaoh said, "I will let you go to offer sacrifices to the Lord, your God, in the desert, but you must not go very far.

Now pray for me." 25 Moses answered, "As soon as I leave you, I will pray to the Lord, and tomorrow the wild animals will leave Pharaoh and his servants and his people. Only be sure that Pharaoh does not act deceitfully again by not letting the people go to offer sacrifices to the Lord." 26 Then Moses left Pharaoh and prayed to the Lord, 27 and the Lord did what Moses asked: The wild animals were removed from Pharaoh and his servants and his people; not one remained. 28 But this time also Pharaoh hardened his heart and would not let the people go.

Converting Physical Reality and Ourselves

We must comprehend that these verses regarding the plagues are teaching us about conversion from negativity to positivity, much as with an operation to cut out cancer—if you are not converting the negativity, then you have not accomplished anything. These plagues were all a conversion of physical reality from negativity into positivity. Yes, there are conditions, and yes, there is a danger in it.

Why do some people walk away with such enthusiasm after hearing the Torah reading on Shabbat? If after hearing this section we do not change, we have not heard the reading. This energy is coming from Zeir Anpin, and we have to hear it three times because the Bible is also here to teach us technology. Only with consistency can this be managed, by using the Three Columns of Right, Left and Central. We have to change ourselves; we have to exercise more of the Three Column System, which begins with restriction. If you are unsure about the power of restriction, I urge you to take the Power of Kabbalah course again. If the idea of restriction is not in our minds each and every single day, then we could be studying for years and still not have mastered the idea. This does not come from being at the Kabbalah Centres many years; it depends on the level of the individual and his or her ability. To the extent that we will hear, we can tap into and capture this energy.

With the story about water turning into blood, why did Rashi bring up the part about the Israelites selling the water? He was sharing with us the idea of restriction, and that everything that goes wrong in our lives is because we are reactive and not proactive. We can capture the power with this reading to exercise restriction in all areas of our lives.

Shemot 9:1 The Lord said to Moses, "Come to Pharaoh and say to him, 'This is what the Lord, the God of the Hebrews, says: "Let My people go, so that they may worship Me." 2 If you refuse to let them go and continue to hold them back, 3 the Hand of the Lord will bring a heavy pestilence on your livestock in the field—on your horses and donkeys and camels and on your cattle and sheep and goats. 4 But the Lord will make a distinction between the livestock of Israel and that of Egypt, so that no animal belonging to the Israelites will die.'" 5 The Lord set a time and said, "Tomorrow the Lord will do this in the land." 6 And the next day the Lord did it: All the livestock of the Egyptians died, but not one animal belonging to the Israelites died. 7 Pharaoh sent men and found that not even one of the animals of the Israelites had died. Yet his heart was unyielding and he would not let the people go. 8 Then the Lord said to Moses and Aaron, "Take handfuls of soot from a furnace and have Moses toss it toward the skies in the presence of Pharaoh. 9 It will become fine dust over the whole land of Egypt, and bubbling boils will break out on men and animals throughout the land of Egypt." 10 So they took soot from a furnace and stood before Pharaoh. Moses tossed it toward the skies, and bubbling boils broke out on men and animals. 11 The magicians could not stand before Moses because of the boils that were on them and on all the Egyptians. 12 But the Lord hardened Pharaoh's heart

and he would not listen to them, just as the Lord had said to Moses. 13 Then the Lord said to Moses, "Get up early in the morning, confront Pharaoh and say to him, 'This is what the Lord, the God of the Hebrews, says: "Let My people go, so that they may worship Me," 14 or this time I will send the full force of My plagues against your heart and against your servants and your people, so you may know that there is no one like Me in all the Earth. 15 For by now I could have stretched out My Hand and struck you and your people with a plague that would have wiped you off the Earth. 16 But I have raised you up for this very purpose, that I might show you My power and that My Name might be proclaimed in all the Earth. 17 You still set yourself against My people and will not let them go. 18 Therefore, at this time tomorrow I will send the worst hailstorm that has ever fallen on Egypt, from the day it was founded till now. 19 Give an order now to bring your livestock and everything you have in the field inside, because the hail will fall on every man and animal that has not been brought in and is still out in the field, and they will die.'" 20 Those of Pharaoh's officials who feared the word of the Lord hurried to bring their slaves and their livestock inside. 21 But those who ignored the word of the Lord left their slaves and livestock in the field. 22 Then the Lord said to Moses, "Stretch out your hand toward the sky so that hail will fall all over Egypt—on men and animals and on everything growing in the fields of Egypt." 23 When Moses stretched out his staff toward the sky, the Lord sent thunder and hail, and lightning flashed down to the ground. So the Lord rained hail on the land of Egypt. 24 There was a heavy hail, and within the hail burning fire fell, none like Egypt had ever seen, since it had first become a nation. 25 Throughout Egypt hail struck everything in the fields—both men and animals; it beat down everything growing in the fields and stripped every tree. 26 Only in the land of Goshen, where the Israelites were, did there fall no hail. 27 Then Pharaoh summoned Moses and Aaron. "This time I have sinned," he said to them. "The Lord is in the right, and I and my people are in the wrong. 28 Pray to the Lord, for we have had enough of the thunder and hail of God. I will let you go; you don't have to stay any longer." 29 Moses replied, "When I have gone out of the city, I will spread out my hands to the Lord. The thunder will stop and there will be no more hail, so you may know that the Earth is the Lord's. 30 But I know that you and your servants still do not fear the Lord, God." 31 The flax and barley were destroyed, since the barley had headed and the flax was in bloom. 32 The wheat and spelt, however, were not destroyed, because they ripen later. 33 Then Moses left Pharaoh and went out of the city. He spread out his hands toward the Lord; the thunder and hail stopped, and the rain no longer poured down on the land. 34 When Pharaoh saw that the

rain and hail and thunder had stopped, he sinned again: He and his servants' hearts became hardened. 35 So Pharaoh's heart was hard and he would not let the Israelites go, just as the Lord had said through Moses.

Conclusion

The portion of Va'era ushers in the story about Passover. We read about the first seven plagues that were thrust upon the Egyptians, and how they suffered, and the power of Moses leading the children of Israel out of Egypt. Unfortunately, this is a corrupted version of the story. The majority of people are stuck in the mainstream consciousness of thinking that given this story, if you are an Israelite, be happy, if you are an Egyptian, be unhappy. We know this is furthest from the truth. We did not come to the War Room on Shabbat just to feel good, where out of all our misery and chaos we can enjoy something a little better by remembering how God was so compassionate through his servant Moses, and that the children of Israel finally raised their heads above that consciousness level of slavery. This whole story in the Bible does not make much sense.

Pharaoh was supposed to be a bright man; let us not forget that this Pharaoh ruled the Middle Kingdom of Egypt and the entire world. What was so difficult about getting rid of a culprit like Moses? Why did Pharaoh not want to get rid of the instigator of all his problems, instead of making demands that the children of Israel make their bricks without the right materials? Getting rid of Moses would have resolved Pharaoh's whole problem. Yet there is no discussion in the Bible at all concerning Moses. He had free reign and could go wherever he wanted in Egypt. Even the Israelites were free to go wherever they wanted too, looking for straw and hay.

What has happened over these 3,400 years? Have we become enlightened people? At no time in history until now have there been chips that could process trillions of bits of data in a second. Were all the previous generations stupid? Whatever answer you can give, there has still been a man on the moon; but computers and many other things have not necessarily improved the life of human beings. Forget that part. All we care about is that we can buy stocks from our own home now; so many things are taking place to change our lifestyle.

Has cancer or any other illness now been reduced to a non-existent malady in our life? Are we gaining control over all these forms of chaos? Of course we are not. For 3,400 years, people have read this story. There was a time when all Jews went to synagogue. They were more learned than we are today. We learn from all the sages throughout the centuries, but we do not have people of this stature today. Today, there is no one whose work compares with the scholarship and knowledge of prior times. Even only as recently as 250 years ago, someone was able to create a *golem* (body without a soul)—which is really another form of computer. It goes way back, what is the difference now?

Our answer in Kabbalah is that in this century, for the first time, a breakthrough has been accomplished by making Kabbalah available to all people. All the concepts that we suddenly find, concepts that did not exist in the past, have become a reality. For me, this is somewhat of an explanation because I have not found any other.

Therefore, this story is a revelation. Forget the literal stories of the Bible, they are meaningless, they are contradictory, and sometimes they are even corrupt. But they are also a form of communication that enables people to grasp the awesome thoughts that are filtered through them.

As Rav Shimon declares many times in the Zohar, the stories in the Bible do not have any significance—this is shattering news for the mainstream religions. Can you imagine mainstream Jews getting up and complaining to Silicon Valley for the discovery of all this new technology—do you hear one peep from them? Not one. No one has any objection to Silicon Valley uncovering unprecedented knowledge, but Kabbalah! What we have endured over the past 88 years or so is mind-boggling. But nobody complains about Silicon Valley.

Therefore, this Shabbat is indeed one of the most powerful days of the year to bring us closer to a chaos-free world. We are privileged to be living in the Age of Aquarius, and after all my years of involvement in Kabbalah, for the first time I noticed something about the planet Saturn. I have read the same paragraph in the *Sefer Yetzirah* ("Book of Formation") many times but I did not notice it before because this was the right moment, the time has come to understand it. Abraham the patriarch injected a word into the explanation of the planet Saturn, which rules the month of Aquarius—it was the word "life." This is the only place in this book, which is not a big book, that the word "life" is mentioned. Herein lies the importance of Va'era in the Book of Shemot.

BOOK OF SHEMOT:

Portion of Bo

PORTION OF BO

Shemot 10:1 Then the Lord said to Moses, "Come to Pharaoh, for I have hardened his heart and the hearts of his servants so that I may perform these miraculous signs of Mine among him; 2 that you may tell your children and grandchildren how I dealt harshly with the Egyptians and how I performed My signs among them, and that you may know that I am the Lord."

Bo, Come to Where God is

The portion of Bo was my personal entrance into the world of truth. I derived the initial idea of what truth was from the first verse in this section. I discovered that the Hebrew word *bo*, which actually means "*come*," is translated in this portion as "*go*." What other way could there be to validate the word *bo*? *Bo* does not have any other meaning except "come," and certainly it does not mean the opposite. The word "go" in Hebrew is *lech*. I had not heard this translation questioned before the Zohar was presented to me many years ago. Despite having been written 1,400 years after the event on Mount Sinai, the Zohar concluded that we cannot change a word of the Bible; we cannot manipulate the words to come to a logical understanding of the stories. The Zohar says that even after 3,400 years of a corruption in the translation, it is difficult for us to let go. This translation persists today, and *bo* is still presented as "go."

From this we learn one of the basic principles in Kabbalah, a principle not easy to grasp. It is very difficult, not for us to hear

143

and understand what is said but for it to become a part of our essence. The principle is this: Everything that takes place in the physical, material world is only the effect of a prior thought, a prior occurrence, a prior cause in the non-physical, immaterial world. This is the first lesson we should have all learned in Kabbalah. For example, our hand will not go up or down without the prior thought of moving it up and down. Thought is the motivation in this world, and it alone is what initiates an action. Nothing of a physical nature determines action. We put something into motion physically by the thought that determines this motion. The original force behind all physical movement must originate in the immaterial and non-physical realm.

In this verse, God told Moses "come to where I am," to where God is. Come up to where he, Moses, could fight Pharaoh in consciousness. We can never eliminate chaos on the physical level; only on the metaphysical realm can this be achieved. Only by coming to God could Moses then destroy Pharaoh in the physical realm. To fully destroy negativity we must get to the root. Just getting rid of the negative person has never been the answer. We have seen this time and time again throughout history. World War II was supposed to be the war to end all wars, and yet, as I read in the newspaper today, at any one moment in time there are 36 wars going on somewhere in the world.

As we have learned in the previous two portions of the Book of Shemot, we are not discussing Pharaoh or the Egyptians; we are discussing the chaos that persists in the world. The 72 Names of God—*Mem, Tzadik, Resh*—will help remove chaos.

Science is looking for a connection between the mind and physicality, but this bridge has not been found yet. Kabbalists have found the bridge; it is mind over matter. Therefore, what God is telling Moses to do is to get to the root of chaos. Let us not treat chaos superficially; we need the metaphysical root not the seed of physicality. Its roots go beyond, just as the root of cancer often goes 30 years back. We need to deal with cancer at this level, at the level before there is a physical expression of any disease or ailment. How do we do that? We go back to the metaphysical root.

This is what the Bible is teaching us. God is telling us, *Bo*: "Come with Me to where I am. I am at a non-physical performing level." God is above the level of anything of a physical nature. So when God said: "Come to Pharaoh," He meant "Come with Me into this realm above physical nature because it is the only realm where we can eliminate chaos."

All Matters that Pertain to Physical Existence are an Illusion

When the Bible says, *Bo el Paro* (Come to Pharaoh), Moses is in essence being told the physical world that we observe is one of total illusion. This is the theme of the entire portion. The world we experience today, the world of sickness, accidents, and every other form of chaos is all an illusion. And yet who in his right mind will deal with sickness as an illusion? Sickness is something very real. When an individual experiences pain and cannot walk it is very real.

But from this verse we learn that all matters pertaining to physical existence are an illusion. It is not only Rav Shimon bar Yochai who says that this world is an illusion; physicists also agree that this world, as we see it, as we feel it with the five senses, is an illusion. In other words, the real world, the 99 percent of existence, is in the metaphysical realm, the realm that we cannot see or observe. We know that with cancer, it may have started 10, 15, or even 20 years prior. What the doctor observes 20 years later is already the manifestation. Medical science agrees that cancer begins on a level that is not observable.

If we stop for a moment and consider everything around us, we will notice that we really have no control over most things that occur in our daily life. This is because the things that ultimately affect us began long before we could observe them. Going on this premise, that the true reality is the world we do not see, how can we deal with it if we cannot observe it?

We know that Pharaoh was the embodiment of all evil in the entire world. And evil here does not mean bad but rather it refers to illness, accidents, anything that constitutes chaos. According to Rav Shimon, when God told Moses to "Come to Pharaoh," God was saying, if we want to deal with anything in our lives, we have to deal with it at its source. If Moses wanted to defeat Pharaoh, he would have to come up into the world of the metaphysical realm, the world that is unseen. There and only there would he be able to deal with Pharaoh. This lesson applies to us today because from this section we understand that we cannot eradicate any form of chaos on this physical level.

The Hebrew Letters are the Means to Control Physical Reality

In this same verse it says: "I have hardened his heart, and also the heart of his servants so that I might show you My signs in the midst of them." Rav Isaac Luria (the Ari) questions why the Bible says "My signs." What signs? Is it a sign on the road? Why not simply say that I'm going to continue to bring some more plagues on Pharaoh? In studying the Zohar and Kabbalah, we learn how to observe the internal and hidden meaning of these verses. The word *ototai* translated as "My signs" comes from the Hebrew word *ot*, which means "letter."

When the Bible discusses the Fourth Day of Creation in Genesis 1: 14, it states, "And the Lord said, 'Let there be lights in the firmament of the Heavens to divide the day from night, and let them be for *signs*.'" Again, the word used is *l'otot*. The Zohar explains that *otot* is not referring to "signs" as the Hebrew word for "sign" is *shelet*. Rav Shimon explains that we cannot change any of the literal meanings of the words because we do not understand their contextual meaning.

What is so significant about these letters? The answer is simple. As we have learned in the study of Kabbalah, by making use of the Hebrew *Alef-Bet* one can come to control one's life, one can come to control healing, and anything that exists on this physical level. Without making use of the *Alef-Bet*, we have absolutely no control.

No Such Thing as Lucky or Unlucky

In a situation where you have two people with the same condition who are given the same treatment but one recovers and the other does not, we ask: "Why?" It has much to do with other factors, factors which are not observable. It has to do with particular months where the cosmic conditions make people more vulnerable than other months. If one does not know how to watch over oneself, negative energy can attach to an individual. If one does not know how to prevent this negative energy from attaching, then that individual will get sick or have an accident. According to Kabbalah, there is no such thing as being lucky or unlucky. When someone is vulnerable, they are exposed to the unseen influences of negative energy.

At the time of the exodus, for the first time in history, humankind was given the opportunity to take control over their lives. This is called freedom; it is freedom from fear, freedom from uncertainty. Freedom means you have control over your life. The story of the exodus is completely concealed. The Book of Shemot is intended to teach the whole world how we can take control over evil, over Egypt. Yet if we were to ask most people in the world if they had control over their lives the answer would be: "No."

This whole business of the plagues then, of leaving Egypt, and the Splitting of the Red Sea, was not for the Israelites. The story represents teachings that are meant to help all of humanity for all time, whether at the time of the exodus or at some future date. The Israelites then were provided, as we are today, with a system by which we can always enjoy freedom.

Physicians today say that the biggest problem a cancer patient faces is the fear that they have an enemy within, and that this enemy is eating away inside them every single day. They are living with an enemy that is not somewhere out there but deep within them.

What was significant in Egypt was not the fact that the plagues were being forced upon the Egyptians. Their suffering was not the reason they recognized that there is a God. The significance of the exodus was that the Egyptians observed that the Israelites were separated from all that was happening. None of the plagues affected the Israelites. This made a significant impression on the Egyptians. The fact that the Israelites would have been slaughtered and persecuted would not have made any impression. These are just things that come and go.

You can never capture or remove darkness by force. You create Light. What they observed was that there was a secret the Israelites were in possession of that brought about a condition where they were unaffected by everything that affected the Egyptians. The Israelites were not affected by the blood. Their water was still water. Everything that was evil was prevented from entering into the realm of what was called the Israelite. Therefore, water for the Israelite could not become contaminated because there was a security shield around them which was accomplished by the Shemot, the Names.

The Bible here is not speaking about "signs" but about "letters." God hardened the heart of Pharaoh so he would now understand that there is something beyond his control. Where previously he controlled the whole world—the physical universe, according to the Zohar, suddenly here Pharaoh had absolutely no control over it.

The water turned into blood and it remained blood, except for the Israelites. Pharaoh had no control. With the advent of the exodus, control of evil came to an end. Pharaoh then understood that there was something more than Elohim. There is the Lightforce of God, the Tetragrammaton—*Yud*, *Hei*, *Vav*, and *Hei*.

Pharaoh came to understand that he had no control over the Tetragrammaton. He had no control because *Elohim* also has two parts. There is *Elohim*, and then there is *Elohim Acherim* meaning other gods. In other words, the level of consciousness that is *Elohim* was a level where Pharaoh had control. However, he had no dominion at the level of *Yud*, *Hei*, *Vav*, and *Hei*. With the Hebrew letters, the *Shemot*, and the power of the *Alef-Bet*, a security shield was created and the Tetragrammaton would now rule. The Israelites were not vulnerable anymore. There was no room for evil to come in, whatever evil means.

Fear was what made Pharaoh understand that there was another force, a force that would destroy him. It was not the plagues that could take the Israelites out of Egypt; it was the Names, the *Shemot*.

3 So Moses and Aaron went to Pharaoh and said to him, "This is what the Lord, the God of the Hebrews, says: 'How long will you refuse to humble yourself before Me? Let My people go, so that they may worship Me. 4 If you refuse to let them go, tomorrow I will bring locusts into your borders. 5 They will cover the face of the ground so that it cannot be seen. They will devour what you have left after the hail, including every tree that is growing in your fields. 6 They will fill your houses and those of all your servants and all the Egyptians—something neither your fathers nor your forefathers have ever seen from the day they settled in this land till now.'" Then Moses turned and left Pharaoh. 7 Pharaoh's servants said to him, "How long will this man be a snare to us? Let the people go, so that they may worship the Lord, their God. Do you not yet realize that Egypt is lost?" 8 Then Moses and Aaron were brought back to Pharaoh. "Go, worship the Lord, your God," he said. "But just who will be going?" 9 Moses answered, "We will go with our young and old, with our sons and daughters, and with our flocks and herds, because we are to celebrate a festival to the Lord." 10 Pharaoh said, "The Lord be with you—if I let you go, along with your women and children! Clearly you are bent on evil. 11 No! Have only the men go; and worship the Lord, since that's what you have been asking for." Then they were driven out of Pharaoh's presence. 12 And the Lord said to Moses, "Stretch

out your hand over Egypt so that locusts will swarm over the land of Egypt and devour everything growing in the land, everything left by the hail." 13 So Moses stretched out his staff over Egypt, and the Lord made a mighty wind blow across the land all that day and all that night. By morning the wind had brought the locusts. 14 They invaded all Egypt and settled down in every area of the country in great numbers. Never before had there been such a heavy plague of locusts nor will there ever be again. 15 The land became dark as they devoured everything growing in the fields and the fruit on the trees – all that was left after the hail. Nothing green remained on tree or plant in all the land of Egypt. 16 Pharaoh quickly summoned Moses and Aaron and said, "I have sinned against the Lord, your God and against you. 17 Now forgive my sin once more and pray to the Lord, your God, to just take this death from me."

The Nature of the Desire to Receive for Oneself Alone

If you look closely at the first two verses of this portion, you will notice that the Lord did not tell Moses what plague He was going to bring on the Egyptians. All of the commentators struggle with why the Lord did not tell Moses which plague it would be.

So how did Moses know that God meant the plague of locusts? Some say that there was a private conversation not recorded in the Bible, and that Moses understood the next plague would have to be the plague of the locusts.

The holiday of Passover revolves around *matzah*. What is *matzah*? It is made from wheat. We also learn that the reason the Israelites did not permit the bread to rise was that they were making an attempt to restrict the Desire to Receive because there is nothing in this world that expands by itself like bread.

We know that if you put out a piece of meat for several days, the meat shrinks; and if we leave water in a glass for several days, it evaporates. Things do not expand; things do not get bigger as a natural consequence. The only substance in this universe that expands on its own is dough.

The Desire to Receive always expands in a person. This comes naturally to everyone, since we never stop thinking of what we need, of what we want. We are always involved with or consumed by what tomorrow will bring for us. Therefore, the whole idea of *matzah* was to restrict the Desire to Receive.

Matzah is wheat, which grows from the ground. When God told Moses "Come to Pharaoh," God was telling him what will come next. But how? We have already learned that *Bo el Paro* means "Come up with Me, and I will show you how we can control the Desire to Receive for Oneself Alone." The Desire to Receive is not evil by and of itself. In fact, the Desire to Receive is what makes people move. When people want something, they have to go get it, and thus they have to work for it. However, when we desire only for ourselves, this is evil. The power of the Desire to Receive for Oneself Alone expands on its own. No one has to tell me that tomorrow I will need bread. The body speaks by itself, alone. It does not need any support from anyone to tell us that we constantly need something, be it clothing or food or water. Needs, necessities, and desires are like bread; they expand on their own.

The Zohar says that Pharaoh was the epitome of the Desire to Receive for Oneself Alone. God said there is only one way we are going to defeat Pharaoh and that is to put the control of the Desire to Receive onto ourselves, the Israelites, by removing everything the Egyptian held in high esteem, which is the power of the Earth. What is the power of Earth? Gravity—the Desire to Receive for Oneself Alone. It pulls toward itself. Yet can we see it? Can we feel it? No.

Therefore, for the first time, everything that emerged from the ground would come to an end. When God said, "*Bo el Paro*," Moses understood what these signs were all about. They all led to one thing: the destruction of the Desire to Receive for Oneself Alone because that was the power of the Egyptians, and the way they controlled the whole world.

The ancient Egyptians knew the art of mummification—how to preserve the power of the body as opposed to the power of the soul. The soul has a Desire to Share. What is the power of the body? One thing: Me! This is what forces us to act, day in and day out. It is an expansion. The body is powerful. The Egyptians could preserve a body, so that it would never die.

No nation in the world, not even the Egyptians themselves, after the time of exodus had the knowledge of how to create mummification in bodies. It was over with. It was destroyed. When this locust plague came, it was the end. When the locusts came they destroyed every aspect of the Desire to Receive. Pharaoh's power was broken by the locusts. They destroyed everything that emerged from the ground. The ground was no longer the force for Egyptians. Moses first accomplished the demise of Pharaoh on the Upper Level, and then along came the locusts and finished the job on this 1 Percent Illusionary Level.

We learn from the Bible that it is not force that wipes out darkness. It is only Light that can remove negativity, and this removal does not happen as a result of a battle between Light and darkness. When there is Light, there is no more darkness. We do not have to tell the darkness to go because what is being illuminated is the Light that was there before the darkness occurred.

18 Moses then left Pharaoh and prayed to the Lord. 19 And the Lord changed the wind to a very strong seaward wind, which caught up the locusts and carried them into the Red Sea. Not a locust was left anywhere in Egypt. 20 But the Lord hardened Pharaoh's heart, and he would not let the Israelites go. 21 Then the Lord said to Moses, "Stretch out your hand toward the sky so that darkness will spread over Egypt—darkness that can be felt." 22 So Moses stretched out his hand toward the sky, and total darkness covered all Egypt for three days. 23 No one could see anyone else or leave his place for three days. Yet all the Israelites had light in the places where they lived.

Darkness Meant the Egyptians Lost All Consciousness and All Knowledge

In the Plague of Darkness there was darkness for the Egyptians and Light for the Israelites. The Egyptians' experience was so extreme that they could not get up from their chairs. This was a plague.

Rav Isaac Luria (the Ari) claims that darkness is an illusion. We speak so much about illusion and yet, for many of us, when the room is lit we can see; and when the room is dark, we can no longer see. In this section, we are not discussing physical sight but rather the consciousness beyond physical eyesight. When people make mistakes in life does it mean they do not see well, that they have bad eyesight? No. We make mistakes because we do not see all the circumstances that surround a particular condition or situation.

There is not enough intelligence or insight. These are the factors that constitute seeing or blindness, darkness or Light.

When the Lord told Moses to create this kind of darkness, it was not a physical darkness that would be a problem for the Egyptians. If God had told Moses to go to the Egyptians and say, "I'm bringing a plague of darkness, and you will not be able to see anything. There will be no light. The candles cannot be lit," it would not have impressed the Egyptians at all. Thus there was no purpose in God telling Moses to go to Pharaoh and tell him, "We're bringing a plague of darkness." Physical darkness was not a plague.

A plague is something unknown that strikes some people and not others. In the case of the Black Plague, which devastated a third of the European population, it was not the extreme number of deaths that made it a plague, but rather the fear of it that ensued as no one knew who would be struck down next. It was an unseen, unknown force that was causing death and destruction in a manner that was abnormal.

Death is not a plague. The plague is the unseen factor—a fear of the unknown. They could not attribute the cause to something that they could identify. The fear was to be struck down by something that they had no control over.

What was the fear surrounding the plague of darkness? It was that some people were struck with Light, and some people were struck with darkness. The Egyptians could now understand that there is an unseen cause. How could there be light in one part of the room, and darkness in another part of the same room?

In other words, if there was an Egyptian sitting together with an Israelite in the same room, the Egyptian would experience darkness, and at the same time understand that the Israelite had light. This was the significant aspect of the plague, and it became a trauma for the Egyptian because this was something plaguing him that not everyone was undergoing. There was a force that was selecting who would be engulfed in darkness and who in light. There was uncertainty around who was going to be selected. A similar selection process took place in concentration camps. Everyone would line up with the knowledge that there was a selection that would take place and lead some to live and some to die. What were the criteria? How was the selection made? There was an unbearable fear as one approached the person who would make the selection. The fear of not knowing is why it is called a plague.

What does it mean that the Egyptians could not get up? They lost all capacity of consciousness. It was not because they were starved or did not eat; and it did not mean they could not function. The Egyptians lost all form of consciousness. This was the plague. It was total darkness. When someone has a problem—in the family or in a business—a problem they cannot think or see how to solve, then nothing any longer exists for them.

What happened in Egypt was that the Egyptians were brought to the point where they were blank; they saw nothing and felt nothing. They realized there was no Light, there was no illumination. All of the knowledge they possessed yesterday they now forgot. All of the thinking processes they usually made use of ceased to exist. There was a total blackout of their consciousness. That was the fear.

They were however able to see and realize that there was consciousness among the Israelites. The Israelites were totally conscious; their minds were functioning.

24 Then Pharaoh summoned Moses and said, "Go, worship the Lord; only leave your flocks and herds behind – your families may join you." 25 But Moses said, "You must allow us to have sacrifices and burnt offerings to present to the Lord our God. 26 Our livestock too must go with us; not a hoof is to be left behind. We have to use some of them in worshiping the Lord our God, and until we get there we will not know what we are to use to worship the Lord." 27 But the Lord hardened Pharaoh's heart, and he was not willing to let them go. 28 Pharaoh said to Moses, "Get out of my sight! Make sure you do not appear before me again! The day you see my face you will die." 29 "Just as you say," Moses replied, "I will never appear before you again."

Pharaoh and the Cattle

What was the whole discussion between Moses and Pharaoh about taking the cattle or not, and the offerings to God? Pharaoh was beaten with a terrible plague and now he was arguing to keep the cattle? Pharaoh understood the technology of the food chain and how to inject negativity into it. He would pollute the cattle, food and then the Israelites would come back to the negativity.

Today, we have people polluting our air, water, and food. This is another reason it is so important today to share the Zohar and Kabbalah Water with the world so as to remove the pollution from the food, air, water, and the whole environment.

Shemot 11:1 The Lord said to Moses, "I will bring one more plague on Pharaoh and on Egypt. After that, he will let you go from here, and when he does, he will drive you out completely. 2 Tell the people that the men should ask their neighbors and the women should ask their neighbors for articles of silver and gold." 3 The Lord made the Egyptians favorably disposed toward the people, and Moses himself was highly regarded in Egypt by Pharaoh's servants and by the people.

What it Means to Borrow

What is this section all about? First of all, what are the Israelites going to do with gold and silver in the wilderness? Were they just going to hoard it? Were they going to corner the market? There was no market. The Israelites now had all the gold and silver in the whole world; there was no more gold and silver left. But what strikes me most is the English translation, which is a corruption. The English translation of the Bible says, "And let them ask every man of his neighbor." The Hebrew word used in the Bible is *yishalu* (ישאלו), derived from the word *lishol* (לשאול), which means "borrow" not "ask." God told the Israelites to borrow the gold and silver; this is what the Bible says, and we cannot change that.

What does the Bible mean when it says the Israelites should borrow? Were they supposed to pay it back some time in the future? The answer is that God knew the nature of humanity. The reference to borrowing and not taking is to teach us that the money we have is always borrowed, and what we do with it will determine if it remains with us or not. We have to treat money as a vehicle and as a channel, not as an end game. It is a means, not an end. It is not about the accumulation of money. Money is not something we possess; money is something we make use of. Whether we borrow something or own it—a car or a mixer—and make use of it, it is not the fact of possession that makes it a functional item.

4 So Moses said, "This is what the Lord says: 'About midnight I will go throughout Egypt 5 and every firstborn son in Egypt will die, from the firstborn son of Pharaoh, who sits on the throne, to the firstborn son of the slave girl, who is at her hand mill, and all the firstborn of the cattle. 6 There will be a loud cry throughout Egypt—worse than there has ever been or ever will be again. 7 But among the Israelites not a dog will bark at any man or animal. Then you will know that the Lord makes a distinction between Egypt and Israel.

The Angel of Death

In the portion of Bo we have the removal of the final three stages of negativity. The higher the level, the more serious the energy of chaos. The Zohar states clearly that no one dies from a heart attack, no one dies from cirrhosis of the liver, no one dies from a brain tumor, and no one dies according to any medical statement on a death certificate that claims to indicate the true cause of death. The Zohar says that we cannot see the cause of death through physical means. This was written 2,000 years ago, long before its time, even though the medical profession still maintains that only a physician is able to provide the cause of death. The Zohar teaches that there is a force of death known as the *Malach haMavet* (Angel of Death).

In art and literature we have depicted angels as beautiful winged creatures—and then I have to spoil this charming image by mentioning the Angel of Death. We are not taught about angels of death. Are angels of death as evil as they sound? Within the study of Kabbalah the definition or explanation of the nature of an angel is that it is a channel for particular energies that can be positive or negative—and it is the same with the Angel of Death.

The reason we die, according to the Zohar, is that when we become vulnerable, we are open to the entry of the Angel of Death into our lives, into our families, and into our environment. Then the Angel of Death will choose how he will execute his victim. He may choose the heart, he may choose the brain, he may choose the liver. The Angel of Death draws to itself and, ultimately, the victim succumbs.

8 All these officials of yours will come to me, bowing down before me and saying, "Go, you and all the people who follow you!" After that I will leave."' Then Moses, hot with anger, left Pharaoh. 9 The Lord had said to Moses, "Pharaoh will refuse to listen to you—so that my wonders may be multiplied in Egypt." 10 Moses and Aaron performed all these wonders before Pharaoh, but the Lord hardened Pharaoh's heart, and he would not let the Israelites go out of his country.

Shemot 12:1 The Lord said to Moses and Aaron in Egypt, 2 "This month is to be for you the first month, the first of the months of the year.

The New Moon

The Zohar says that God gives us a precept: "This month is ours." There is plenty of ink spent on this verse but what does this phrase and the precept of Blessing the New Moon have to do with going out of Egypt? Does this mean that this month is *actually* ours? Here is the origin of controlling the influences of the stars. We can observe that planetary bodies influence us and the Earth even from extremely long distances; one can recognize the impact of high tides and low tides, which depend on the moon, and the moon can also effect human behavior. In the portion of Bo we are taught about this truth.

The Zohar says we can take control of the forces that virtually compel us to behave in certain ways. There is an old saying, "While the stars may compel, they do not impel"—which means that we can change the influences that extend from negative forces as well as from positive ones. There are good and evil people in this world; so too there are unseen forces that can be positive or negative. All of the celestial influences can be ours to control.

Sanctify the New Moon

We read that when we see a new moon, we must sanctify it and make the new moon holy. Does anyone still do *Kiddush haLevanah* (Sanctify the New Moon)? There is a small segment of Orthodox Jews who do. Any time following the first seven days after the proclamation of the New Moon (Rosh Chodesh), until the 15th day of that lunar month, are the days that we can Sanctify the New Moon. We go outside, look at the moon and say praise. Hardly anyone knows the meaning of it. Within our own circles, we usually do it on Saturday night but it does not have to be then. We do not sanctify the moon literally; instead, we are making a connection, which is another opportunity to take control of the moon because it is a channel to this world. It is not to sanctify but to connect so as to accomplish one objective: to remove chaos, nothing more. Everything, all of the Bible, is about removing chaos and death.

We have all been here in a prior lifetime. Reincarnation makes sense if we reflect on it. How else does God permit a little child to be born blind? The Zohar asks how God permits evil things to happen to little children. We have been taught that we are not supposed to ask questions about the workings of God. However, the Zohar demands that we ask these questions. Why do bad things happen to good people? The process of reincarnation goes a long way to answer these questions. The Zohar says that our actions in a past life can make us vulnerable to chaos in certain months in our current life. Do we have to pay a price in this lifetime for the brutalities of past lives? The Zohar says no, because in each month we are given positive energies (this is the study of astrology). And when we Sanctify the New Moon we are given an opportunity to access positive energies. Though life often appears grim with the degree of chaos that mankind commits and endures, we can keep in mind the rules of the universe, and we use this connection to the New Moon to prevent chaos from wreaking havoc in our lives.

As stated previously, the precept of Sanctifying the New Moon is performed seven days after the new month is proclaimed. We go outside and say a certain prayer to Sanctify the New Moon. This precept was given to the Israelites before the final plague of Slaying of the Firstborn. Why? The answer to this question is quite obvious. The 10th Plague—Slaying of the Firstborn—was the demise, the final devastation of whatever was called Egypt.

In Rav Isaac Luria's Gate of Divine Inspiration, and many other texts, including Abraham the Patriarch's book called the *Sefer Yetzirah* ("Book of Formation"), we learn that the Hebrew letters created the Universe. Before the Israelites could leave Egypt, before they could enjoy what was called the exodus, they would have to have control over their destiny.

There is an unseen influence that can invade us if we are vulnerable and open, and do not have a protection or security shield around us. If we did not create a security shield, we are then vulnerable to all of the effects of the cosmos. We must protect ourselves. The same way as cancer invades some and not others for no apparent reason, which we know is incorrect since nothing happens without a reason; there is a cause for everything that happens.

The Israelites were taught that before they could have actual freedom and leave Egypt, they needed to know the secrets of the cosmos. They had to know about the influences of each month because if they did not have control over unseen influences they would not know how to protect themselves.

The reason they were given this precept of Sanctifying the New Moon before the exodus was because even if the Israelites had left Egypt and gone to an island where no one could harm them, they would never be free people. Because even on an island all by themselves nothing can prevent cancer; nothing can prevent an earthquake; nothing can prevent lightning from striking. So where is the freedom from fear?

Where in the universe can we run to achieve freedom? There is only one place we can run to, to achieve freedom, and that is right where we are. If there is freedom established where you are, you have true freedom. But to seek freedom elsewhere is never achieved because the same uncertainties, the same problems that exist here, can also exist there. What guarantees do you have?

Therefore, before the Israelites could have what is considered to be the exodus, meaning freedom from every fear that people in the world have, they were given the Hebrew letters that we use every month. There are new forces—positive and negative—that operate in each particular month, and the way we protect ourselves is with the *Alef-Bet*. By having a connection with the letters of each month, and with the *Ana Beko'ach*, which we also recite, this provides that kind of protection.

Freedom first is protection from unseen invading influences; without that, there is no protection. Therefore, the Israelites could go out of Egypt, the physical leaving of Egypt, the physical departure from this bondage, only through the Sanctification of the New Moon.

3 Speak to the entire Congregation of Israel, saying that on the tenth day of this month each man is to take a lamb for his family, one for each household. 4 If any household is too small for a whole lamb, they must share one with their nearest neighbor, accounting for each person according to how much of the lamb he would consume. 5 The lamb must be a pure, year-old male lamb, from the lambs and the goats you shall take. 6 You will guard them until the fourteenth day of the month, and slaughter it – the entire assembly of the Congregation of Israel – at twilight. 7 And you shall take from the blood and put it on the two doorposts and on the frame of the houses where the lambs are eaten. 8 And you shall eat the meat on that night roasted over fire, and unleavened bread with bitter herbs you shall eat 9 Do not eat the meat raw or cooked in water, but roast it over the fire— head, legs and inner parts. 10 Do not leave any of it till morning; if some is left till morning, you must burn it. 11 This is how you are to eat it: with your cloak tucked into your belt, your sandals on your feet and your staff in your hand. Eat it in haste; it is the Lord's Passover. 12 I will pass through Egypt on that same night and strike every firstborn in Egypt—both men and animals—and I will bring judgment on all the gods of Egypt. I am the Lord. 13 The blood will be a sign for you on the houses where you are; and when I see the blood, I will pass over you. No deadly plague will touch you when I strike Egypt.

14 This is a day you are to commemorate; for the generations to come you shall celebrate it as a festival to the Lord—a lasting ordinance. 15 For seven days you are to eat unleavened bread, but on the first day you shall remove grain from your houses, for whoever eats anything leavened must be cut off from Israel, from the first day through the seventh day. 16 On the first day hold a sacred assembly, and another one on the seventh day. You shall do no work at all on these days, except to prepare food for everyone to eat—that is all you may do. 17 And you shall guard the unleavened bread, because it was on this very day that I brought your legions out of Egypt. You shall keep this day as a lasting ordinance for the generations to come. 18 From the beginning of the fourteenth day, in the evening, you shall eat unleavened bread until the twenty-first day of the month in the evening. 19 For seven days no grain shall be found in your houses, because anyone who eats that which is leavened shall be cut off from the Congregation of Israel, whether he is a stranger or native-born. 20 Eat nothing that is leavened; in all of your habitations, you shall eat unleavened bread." 21 Then Moses summoned all the elders of Israel and said to them, "Go at once and select a flock for your families and slaughter the Passover lamb. 22 And you shall take a bunch of hyssop, dip it into the blood in the basin and touch it to both sides and the top of the doorframe, with the blood from the basin; and not one

**of you shall go out the door of his house un-
til morning. 23 When the Lord goes through
the land to strike down the Egyptians, He
will see the blood on the top and sides of the
doorframe. And the Lord will pass over that
doorway, and He will not permit the destroy-
er to enter your houses and strike you down.**

Blood on the Doorpost and the Central Column

What was the meaning of the slaughter of the lamb and the
placement of blood on a doorpost? The idea is so bewildering that
I still cannot understand how, so many years later, we still go along
with this story. Nearly the whole world believes in the Bible. Three
major religions have their foundations built upon it, and all believe
that the Israelites were told to literally take the blood and smear it
on the doorpost, so that when the Angel of Death saw the blood
he would not come into the house. As if God did not know who
lived in each house! Why has everyone been accepting this for 3,400
years? Kabbalists do not accept it.

The reason the Israelites were required to sacrifice a lamb and smear
blood on the doorpost was not that the procedure would tell God
who not to kill. What the Bible is teaching us here is that there is a
requirement, one that we learn about in Kabbalah. This teaching is
not available today in those Far Eastern religions that discuss the yin
and yang, the Right and Left. In Kabbalah there is a stress on the
essential Central Column, in addition to the Right and Left.

This is the way the Zohar explains a seemingly nonsensical tradition
of slaughter and blood. It is really about the principle of Restriction.
We could perform all the precepts of the Bible but if we do not treat
others with human dignity we can expect to experience chaos and

to be visited by the Angel of Death. The "plague" of the Killing of the Firstborn was not a plague but rather the opportunity to remove chaos from our lives. The blood on doorposts was not the symbol that God required so that He could be advised where the Israelites lived; it is about the energy of the Central Column. This is the secret behind the removal or prevention of chaos.

On Shabbat, the instrument of the *Berich Shemei*, which is sung before the reading of the Torah Scroll, is our tool to travel back in time to the giving of the Torah on Mount Sinai. When we listen to the portion of Bo, we are given the opportunity to travel back and be present at the original Passover night and awaken the miracle of removing chaos from our lives. On this night, the root of chaos was temporarily eliminated with God's intervention. Both the Talmud and the Zohar say if that one experience had never occurred in time, today we could not contemplate or consider the ruling over chaos. We could never dream of the ridding of the Angel of Death. Once Passover occurred, the bondage was over, the chains that bound the Israelites were broken, which is why the Israelites were in power. In the Kabbalah Centres, we learn the codes of the universe regarding how we can eliminate chaos from our lives.

24 Obey these instructions as a lasting ordinance for you and your descendants. 25 When you enter the land that the Lord will give you as He promised, observe this ceremony. 26 And when your children ask you, 'What does this ceremony mean to you?' 27 tell them, 'It is the Passover sacrifice to the Lord, who passed over the houses of the Israelites in Egypt and spared our homes when He struck down the Egyptians.'" Then the people bowed down and worshiped. 28 The Israelites did just what the Lord commanded Moses and Aaron. 29 At midnight the Lord struck down all the firstborn in Egypt, from the firstborn of Pharaoh, who sat on the throne, to the firstborn of the prisoner, who was in the dungeon, and the firstborn of all the livestock. 30 Pharaoh and all his officials and all the Egyptians got up during the night, and there was a great cry in Egypt, for there was not a house without someone dead. 31 He summoned Moses and Aaron that night and said, "Get up and leave my people, you and the Israelites, and go worship the Lord as you have requested. 32 Take your flocks and herds, as you have said, and go. And also bless me."

The Cosmos at Midnight

When the Lord slew the firstborn, it was exactly at 12 o'clock midnight. The Zohar asks a very simple question: Why did the Slaying of the Firstborn take place in the middle of the night? Why did God not create the phenomenon of the Slaying of the Firstborn during the day? Why did God not slay the Egyptians in broad daylight so everyone could see? Was there something to hide, so that no one knew because at night everyone would be in their homes and could not see?

The Zohar says that Moses used another word when he said when the slaying would take place. He said, "*kachatzot.*" *Kachatzot* in Hebrew means "approximately." Why would Moses say approximately at 12 o'clock midnight? Does God not know when He is going to slay the firstborn? The Zohar says, *Vayehi bachatzi halayla kachatzi haya tzarich lomar o kachatzot.* Moses seems to be saying "approximately." And yet when the Lord slew the firstborn, it says that it took place right smack at 12 o'clock. The commentators ask why Moses used the word *kachatzot*? They suggest it is because if the killing of the firstborn did not happen exactly at 12 o'clock— let's say, it happened at 11 o'clock and 59 minutes or at 12 o'clock and one minute—then maybe Moses was a liar? And what would follow is that then they would say that the slaying of the firstborn was not true. Rav Shimon says this does not sound plausible.

The Zohar goes into great detail about it, and I will take out the essence of this. There is a kabbalistic practice of waking up at 12 o'clock midnight until the rising of the morning star. The Zohar explains that this is the nature of the cosmos: From 12 o'clock midnight onwards, the cosmos is in a state of constant flowing Light, like the circuitry in a lightbulb. This is the reason that the Slaying of the Firstborn could only take place after 12 o'clock and not at 11 o'clock and 59 minutes or during the day.

How Can We Reconcile the Killing of the Firstborn with the Biblical Precept?

How do we reconcile the "murder" of the firstborn when the Bible tells us: "Thou shalt not kill"? Even the Zohar teaches us that when the Israelites passed through the Red Sea and arrived at safety they wanted to sing, and the Lord said to them, "How can you sing when my children are dying?"

Whatever level of consciousness we are at, if someone is of an Israelite consciousness, these are things about others that no one knows for sure. According to Kabbalah, Israelite consciousness contains a greater Desire to Receive, and therefore a greater ability to achieve a higher level of consciousness. But Kabbalah also points out that all individuals are the people of God.

The Israelites at the time of the Splitting of the Red Sea were told not to sing because the Egyptians were drowning. So what are we to understand about what is going on in this portion with the Slaying of the Firstborn?

Says the Zohar, we are not discussing people here. The energy-intelligence, the force behind the Egyptians, was the Desire to Receive for Oneself Alone. The Egyptians brought this force to the world, and it is the way they controlled the world. This was the evil that was instilled in all of humankind, including the Israelite. The Israelite had achieved the 49th Gate of Impurity—such a high level of evil. Were they deserving of leaving Egypt? Of course not. Had they achieved one more level of evil consciousness, they would never have been taken out of Egypt.

When we are discussing the Slaying of the Firstborn, the firstborn had a particular power that all the other Egyptians did not possess. If that force was not broken there would be no freedom in the world. What was taking place here is freedom—freedom from those limitations, freedom of plagues, freedom of illness, freedom of mishaps.

The Egyptians were the most powerful channels in the Universe for this kind of evil. When we discuss the slaying we are not discussing the physical slaying of people. We are discussing the slaying of a force, a power. These Egyptians were not slain. What was slain was the power by which they controlled the world. Whenever the Bible talks about removing or destroying people, it is not referring to physical people. Destroying the human body is not what the Bible is discussing here. Rather it is discussing the evil consciousness that existed only in the firstborn.

The Tenth Plague and Keter

The last three plagues give us a chance to reassert our freedom in the elimination of Satan on all levels. We must take particular notice of the tenth plague, the final stage and Keter, which is the Slaying of the Firstborn. The Zohar carefully indicates that we are not discussing the slaying of people. Both the Zohar and the Talmud tell us that God does not revel in the death of creatures that He created. Therefore, the Zohar provides us with a lengthy explanation, which assists us in understanding that the plague is connected to freedom. Passover is not really about freedom from physical slavery in Egypt. From scripture we learn that the Israelites had it pretty good in Egypt—after all, they were in control of the entire country there. So good did they have it that the Israelites constantly complained to Moses for removing them from Egypt. This is written repeatedly. Therefore we can remove any thought that Passover concerns freedom from physical slavery. It was by no stretch of the imagination like being released from a concentration camp.

We are given the opportunity on Passover, and also with this reading, to remove the seed of chaos from our lives. The kabbalistic philosophy concerning surgery applies: We can remove the physical aspect of something but if the seed is not removed the problem is not gone; nor is anything healed. This is why the kabbalists use the word "seed." While we cannot discern from the seed what exactly the tree will be like—meaning the number of its branches or the sweetness of its fruit—we do have to assume that the entire tree is in the kernel. It is important for progress in the development of our consciousness to be aware that the seed contains everything. For instance, DNA contains everything that will appear concerning an individual.

The Slaying of the Firstborn is the slaying of the root level of Satan. Satan is not in the cancerous tumor; that is not where he resides. That is merely an extension of the chaos that he wields on us.

The Meaning of the Killing of the Firstborn

The last plague was the Killing of the Firstborn of all Egypt. I am a humanitarian, so every time one country bombs another country and innocent people are hurt, it truly bothers me. Yet, here in the portion of Bo, we have God killing the firstborn. What did these firstborn do to enslave the children of Israel? What if a child was only a few days old? What could an infant have done to bring slavery upon the children of Israel? What about the dictate in the Ten Utterances that says, "Thou shall not kill"? Is this not hypocrisy? There are some who believe, and who even instruct us that killing is permissible. They say it is even noble to kill in the Name of God. But all human beings are created by God. There are those who say that the Jewish race is subhuman, so it is not a problem to kill them. Were these the views held by the Israelites about the Egyptians?

I have often been accused of anti-Semitism when I speak in such a way. Yet I have never been accused of such things with regard to the non-Jew. In fact, when I was in Tunisia, wearing a Galabia and *kipa* (skull cap), I walked the streets past Yasser Arafat's palace and yet no one bothered me.

The Light only exists in the Tree of Life (*Etz haChayim*) consciousness, which is the consciousness necessary to remove ourselves from the chaos of the Tree of Knowledge (*Etz haDa'at*) reality. It is easy to view the Bible literally. To accept responsibility for our lives is very uncomfortable. This is why the Bible is the Tree of Knowledge of Good and Evil and the Zohar, which gives us the answers, is the Tree of Life.

The way the Israelite behaves activates the way of the world. When Israelites have unity, the world has peace; if the Israelites have division, the world is also divided. Consider what we are celebrating at Passover. Is it the Killing of the Firstborn, the death of thousands of innocent people? Is this really something to be celebrated? The reason we are able to accept the simple story in the Bible about the killing of people is because we think of them as the enemy, since we recall that the Egyptians inflicted slavery upon the children of Israel. We do not think about the poor Egyptians because it makes us feel uncomfortable. This is the hypocrisy.

33 The Egyptians urged the people to hurry and leave the country. "For otherwise," they said, "we will all die!" 34 So the people took their dough before it had risen, and carried it on their shoulders in kneading troughs wrapped in clothing. 35 The Israelites did as Moses instructed and borrowed from the Egyptians articles of silver and gold and clothing. 36 The Lord had made the Egyptians favorably disposed toward the people, and they gave them what they asked for; so they took advantage of the Egyptians. 37 The Israelites journeyed from Rameses to Succoth. There were about six hundred thousand men on foot, besides women and children. 38 A Mixed Multitude went up with them, as well as large droves of livestock, both flocks and herds. 39 With the dough they had brought from Egypt, they baked cakes of unleavened bread. The dough had not risen because they had been driven out of Egypt and did not have time to prepare food for themselves. 40 Now the length of time the Israelite people lived in Egypt was 430 years. 41 At the end of the 430 years, to the very day, all the Lord's divisions left Egypt. 42 Because the Lord kept vigil that night to bring them out of Egypt, on this night all the Israelites are to keep vigil to honor the Lord for the generations to come. 43 The Lord said to Moses and Aaron, "These are the regulations for the Passover: 'No foreigner is to eat of it. 44 Any slave you have bought may eat of it after you have circumcised him, 45 but a temporary

resident and a hired worker may not eat of it. 46 It must be eaten inside one house; take none of the meat outside the house. Do not break any of the bones. 47 The whole community of Israel must do this. 48 A foreigner living among you who wants to celebrate the Lord's Passover must have all the males in his household circumcised; then he may take part like one born in the land. No uncircumcised male may eat of it. 49 The same law applies to the native-born and to the foreigner living among you.'" 50 All the Israelites did just what the Lord had commanded Moses and Aaron. 51 And on that very day the Lord brought the Israelites out of Egypt by their divisions.

The Israelites Were in No Hurry

We are told that the Israelites rushed out of Egypt. The Bible said they scampered out so fast that they did not have time for the bread to rise—which, incidentally, only takes 18 minutes. Is this why we eat *matzah* as a Passover ritual? The anti-kabbalists made us believe that the Israelites were slaves looking for the first opportunity to flee. But, later in the story, it is written that they left in the morning. Why wait until morning? Why not run off right away?

This further illustrates that Passover is not a celebration of the exodus from Egypt. On a very material, physical level, if we examine scripture closely, it is clearly stated, without any interpretation, that the children of Israel were not interested in leaving Egypt. However, the picture presented to humankind, and accepted by most, is that the Israelites had been tortured. And yet they were in no rush to leave. They took their time and left in the morning.

Does anyone think that when they opened up the gates of Auschwitz, the Jews did not want to leave? The Israelites were almost forced out of Egypt by some character known as Moses, and then they complained incessantly to him for taking them out, indeed they complained for 40 years during their sojourn in the wilderness.

Exodus 13:1 The Lord said to Moses, 2 "Consecrate to Me every firstborn male. The first offspring of every womb among the Israelites belongs to Me, whether man or animal."

Why does Chaos Continue

There is something very strange here in this section. If, as the Zohar says that by the reading of this section we are removing the source of chaos, which is Satan, then why does chaos still appear from year to year? If we have done the job of removing the source of chaos, Satan, then where does the chaos come from?

To answer these questions, I am going to refer to the *Kitvei haAri* ("Writings of the Ari") by Rav Isaac Luria. The answers to these questions are so difficult to comprehend that the first time I was exposed to them, many years ago, I was literally blown away. Incidentally, I am often asked by people, "Why do I need the books of *Kitvei haAri* if I have the Zohar?" My response is, "Why does the U.S. have a missile system if they have the army?" We need the *Kitvei haAri* because it is another aspect of the protection system.

In the *Kitvei haAri*, Volume 14, page 136, there is a lengthy discourse on the *erev rav*, the "evil" people who have been around us for 3,400 years, and as the Zohar and the Ari say, they are the same souls who return again in every generation. The *erev rav* are Jews who have a peculiar feature in their character—to destroy, create chaos, and sow problems. If we are not aware that they exist, we should be.

The Ari describes the argument between Moses and God regarding the *erev rav*. God told Moses not to bring them with the people, stating that it was better for them stay outside the realm of being Israelites. God said to keep them away because their consciousness was not ready to desire the removal of chaos from this world. They still relished misery.

There is an expression "misery loves company." But why does misery in particular love company? There is an innate character within the *erev rav*, who enjoy seeing misery. God told Moses not to bring them in, that to do so would be inviting trouble. But Moses wanted to finish the job quickly; he knew that this great event, the slaying of the seed of chaos, of Satan, would take place, and thereby he hoped he would also eliminate this desire for destruction that exists within the *erev rav*. God said, "No, this would not take place." But Moses wanted to speed up the process, and he almost succeeded.

In a later portion, we read about the golden calf, the instrument created by the people bent on chaos. God told Moses that there are limitations in what he intended to undertake. God did not wish to permit the *erev rav*'s participation in this event of Redemption of the Firstborn (*Pidyon haBen*), so they were not included. They are not Israelites like everyone else.

There are Jewish people who do not recognize the importance of *Pidyon haBen*, the Redemption of the Firstborn, This action removes the seed of death from within the person. At a *Pidyon haBen*, we follow certain steps and criteria to perform this precept, What is important here, is the purpose for which we perform *Pidyon haBen*, and the technology that is a *Pidyon haBen*. The power of *Pidyon haBen* is another kabbalistic tool to remove those seeds that ultimately can develop into death. No one knows when cancer starts; there is no knowledge of its existence in its earliest state. The power to remove death is what we connect to here.

The *erev rav* were excluded because God did not want this intermingling. Therefore when we perform a *Pidyon haBen*, we meditate to keep out those whom we might consider to be evil. We do not publicize a *Pidyon haBen*. With the action of a *Pidyon haBen* we remove every thread of the seed of chaos and death. However, the next day, we might bring it back again. The Ari says the *erev rav* were not included because they would defile and pollute this tool of *Pidyon haBen*. And we can accomplish this same result, the experience of removing death again by hearing this reading of the Bible.

Unfortunately, there are people who wish death on others, and those people are known as *erev rav*. But sometimes *erev rav* is not a group of people, sometimes we can express an aspect of the *erev rav*. Let me explain. Let us say an individual is lacking energy in an aspect of health or any other good thing in life, and that same individual sees someone who may have what he thinks he wants. If that person's thought consciousness is in a state of "why can't I have that energy, that good aspect that another has?" then this is evil eye and this is the *erev rav* within. If we go to that place then we are playing in dangerous territory.

The Ari tells us to keep any aspect of the *erev rav* that exists within us away. We need to stop looking to see what others may possess that we do not. In this way we can protect ourselves from being included in the group called *erev rav*.

When we listen to the portion of Bo on Shabbat we finish the job. But at the same time it is not finished because it can still come back the next day if we somehow cause negative activity around us that could bring on this seed of death again. Then we need another *Pidyon haBen* or Passover event. We do have the tools but we must remember that we can be part of the *erev rav* at any given moment. We do not want death within us anymore.

Even though the seed of Satan and negativity was removed with the Slaying of the Firstborn, we still need the *Pidyon haBen* to manifest this removal of death. It is like removing the residue of negativity after removing its seed.

3 Then Moses said to the people, "Remember this day, the day you came out of Egypt, out of the land of slavery, because the Lord brought you out of it with a mighty hand. Eat nothing containing yeast. 4 Today, in the month of Aviv, you are leaving. 5 When the Lord brings you into the land of the Canaanites, Hittites, Amorites, Hivites, and Jebusites—the land He swore to your forefathers to give you, a land flowing with milk and honey—you are to perform this ceremony in this month: 6 For seven days eat unleavened bread and on the seventh day hold a festival to the Lord. 7 Eat unleavened bread during those seven days; nothing with yeast in it is to be seen among you, nor shall any grain be seen anywhere within your borders. 8 On that day tell your son, 'I do this because of what the Lord did for me when I came out of Egypt.' 9 This observance will be for you like a sign on your hand and a reminder on your forehead that the law of the Lord is to be on your lips. For the Lord brought you out of Egypt with His Mighty Hand. 10 You must keep this ordinance at the appointed time year after year.

The Nature of Freedom

After 3,400 years we still celebrate the exodus from Egypt and the freedom of the children of Israel. But what is freedom? The Israelites did not want to leave Egypt. On their 40-year journey in the wilderness the Israelites pleaded with Moses to return them to the land of their "slavery."

The freedom of the exodus was freedom from Satan; this is the true purpose of Passover according to the Zohar. Humankind was given an understanding on how to remove the Angel of Death but because of our ignorance chaos persists—even though, throughout our lives, God has given us countless opportunities for change. Some will say I am trying to break up their family reunion by suggesting that the Pesach (Passover) connection is a powerful technology and not a family dinner. Why is it that out of 365 days in a year the family can only get together on this day?

Until we can break the back of Satan, we will not have a chance to escape chaos, which is what Egypt represents. In the Kabbalah Centres we learn about how to use the tools of the Holy Names to keep chaos away. When we bring in the Light, the darkness and chaos have no ability to enter. We are getting at the root of the Satan.

When people get sick the doctors provide various types of treatment, from drugs to surgery. Even though doctors are well intentioned, they are not always right and not always sure what the effects of their treatments will be, if there are any. As the Zohar says, "the road to Hell is paved with good intentions." We have been given the tools from the Zohar and the sages of Kabbalah, and we know that Rav Shimon did not recommend anything that he was not certain was right and would help. He said that the proof is in the pudding, meaning, of course, the proof is in the results.

We have to look at this portion with a different frame of reference. We need to understand that it is our opportunity to extricate ourselves from chaos. This is the purpose of Passover. The children of Israel did not leave Egypt in their consciousness; they stayed in the *Etz haDa'at* (Tree of Knowledge) consciousness, meaning the world of ups and downs. There have always been good days and bad days; chaos has existed since the time of Adam and Eve. The Bible's exodus story is about the children of Israel physically leaving Egypt. They could not be convinced about mind over matter—which is the ability to control their lives.

People will hold onto their chaos and sadness "for all the good reasons." The Kabbalah Centres' goal is to raise the consciousness of all humanity to know that it is possible to control physicality, to remove chaos.

Why did the children of Israel at the time of the exodus not want to break or destroy the physical limitations? Did they not see the miracles of the ten plagues? It was because it requires some effort to understand the tools and create miracles. Ultimately chaos will come in unless we connect to the Lightforce of God.

Because we have the ability to scan the Zohar today, we can remove the final chaos, use the 72 Names of God and all the Holy Name combinations to re-enact the exodus. Through the Hebrew words of the Torah Scroll, and the Zohar, we draw the Lightforce and shatter the darkness of Satan. In Egypt, the totality of the Lightforce came in to take the children of Israel out of chaos. Moses told Rav Shimon that only through the Zohar, which is the *Etz haChayim* (Tree of Life), can we remove chaos.

The phrase "exodus from Egypt" appears fifty times in the Torah Scroll, and we know that is a conscious communication, for the number fifty is a connection to the Sefira of Binah, and it represents jubilee and freedom.

Breaking Down the Impure System through the Plagues

We know that for everything that exists in the Pure System there is something that corresponds to it in the Impure System. The first seven plagues we read about in the portion of Va'era were connected to the lower Seven Sefirot of Chesed, Gevurah, Tiferet, Netzach, Hod, Yesod, and Malchut. In the portion of Bo, we have the final three plagues, which connect us to the Upper Three Sefirot of Keter, Chochmah, and Binah. All these plagues were used to break the energy of Satan, the Impure System.

We have the chance, with our connection to the reading of Bo on Shabbat, to break chaos and limitations and to manifest mind over matter. Scientists know that this is possible in theory but they do not have the tools to manifest it. We know that with the tools of Kabbalah these concepts will become manifest in the physical world.

11 After the Lord brings you into the land of the Canaanites and gives it to you, as He promised on oath to you and your forefathers, 12 you are to give over to the Lord the first offspring of every womb. All the firstborn males of your livestock belong to the Lord. 13 Redeem with a lamb every firstborn donkey, but if you do not redeem it, break its neck. Redeem every firstborn among your sons. 14 In days to come, when your son asks you, 'What does this mean?' say to him, 'With a mighty hand the Lord brought us out of Egypt, out of the land of slavery. 15 When Pharaoh stubbornly refused to let us go, the Lord killed every firstborn in Egypt, from the firstborn human to the firstborn animal. This is why I sacrifice to the Lord the first male offspring of every womb and redeem each of my firstborn sons.' 16 And it will be like a sign on your hand and a symbol on your forehead that the Lord brought us out of Egypt with His Mighty Hand."

Sacrifice or Murder?

Although this is not a plague, we have used that term for 3,400 years, so I will go along with it and use the word plague. Regarding the last plague, which was the Killing of the Firstborn, was this a victory for the children of Israel? We have been told for 3,400 years that the Bible says the Egyptians were brutal people, who murdered and treated these children of Israel poorly, and we had to stop them by getting rid of them, and that was why in every Egyptian

household the firstborn or oldest male was eliminated. Is this why
we celebrate Passover?

Not at the Kabbalah Centres; we do not celebrate for that reason,
since we know that murder is murder and there is no justification
for murder. Therefore, concludes the Zohar, what happened that
evening when the Angel of Death passed over the houses was
something entirely different.

According to the literal translation of the Bible, it says that Pharaoh,
within his own household, suffered the Killing of the Firstborn. All
the Egyptians came to ask him how long he was going to keep the
children of Israel locked up in bondage?

The Zohar says this is not the story. The build-up of these plagues
was for only one purpose: to remove the Angel of Death, so that
this causal level of chaos be taken from the universe—this is
why it was slain. The Zohar asks how we know that this is the
interpretation, and then the Zohar itself answers that in this portion
there is a very strange precept. God said, "Redeem unto me all of
your firstborn sons." Before studying Kabbalah, I did not know
that this precept was not given to the *erev rav* as well. The precept
of Redemption of the First Born (*Pidyon haBen*) is uncommon
even for many Jews. What does redemption of the firstborn mean
and how is this connected to the night of Passover? According to
the Zohar, the reason we perform a *Pidyon haBen* on a male infant
is that this child is born with two energies. When Rav Shimon
explained this, he was before his time, and when God gave this
precept it was not intended to be another burdensome part of
religion. The *Pidyon haBen* is a tool that assists us in the work of
ridding ourselves of the Angel of Death—and ultimately forever.

Those of us who have studied in the Kabbalah Centres know we do
not come to Passover to celebrate the freedom that the children of

Israel experienced in leaving Egypt because we know that they did not want to leave. For forty years in the wilderness they complained to Moses about why he brought them into this forsaken land when they enjoyed the food of Egypt.

So the freedom we are discussing was not a physical freedom, it was a freedom from chaos. The Zohar says that chaos persists because of humankind's ignorance. God will not forsake us. He gave us the opportunity to remove the business of heart attacks, brain tumors, and all the other forms of chaos we can think of from our lives. We come to the Kabbalah Centres on Shabbat not just to pay a courtesy call or to follow the tradition of listening to the Torah Scroll. We come here for only one thing: the removal of chaos.

If, however, tomorrow we go back to treating people with anything less than human dignity—we become vulnerable and permit chaos to come back into our life. This is the one requirement.

The Secret Workings of Pidyon haBen

Remember the firstborn of all Egypt were put to death on the first night of Passover. They died back then, therefore we now perform a ritual known as *Pidyon haBen* (Redemption of the First Born), which as I have noted previously has almost been completely abandoned by other traditions.

What struck me within the Writings of the Ari was that Rav Isaac Luria gleans from the Bible that the precept concerning the Redemption of the Firstborn was not given to the *erev rav* (the anti-kabbalists). Were they Jewish? Yes, so why was the *Pidyon haBen* not given to them? The Ari explains that it was because these people, the *erev rav* or mixed multitude, are evil.

The idea of the *Pidyon haBen* and its ramifications is so profound and mind-boggling. The Zohar says that death lurks within our system; death does not come at the point of death. Something leads up to that point. A person does not die suddenly or even accidentally.

As we said about the phrase *Bo el Paro*, nothing happens with its cause on a physical level. Even an accidental death, such as a fatal car accident. Nothing is determined in the physical sphere without exception. We are our own cause and effect. We are the only ones responsible for our actions and their outcomes.

The anti-kabbalists have done a good job getting us to focus on whose fault it is: The other guy, the one who pulled the trigger, the one who stole my money; it was most certainly not my fault, right? The anti-kabbalists were able to take a billion people and make them think that someone else is responsible for what happens in their own lives.

We at the Kabbalah Centres are trying to undo this. The Zohar says that *Pidyon HaBen* provides us with an opportunity to remove the death that might have established itself within us, before it is manifested.

This does not mean that tomorrow we might not create another reason for the cause of this energy force known as death, in whatever form Satan chooses, to enter our system. Death did not start in one moment. It starts before. It starts when we created an opening for the energy known as death to enter our system.

According to the Zohar, when we perform the Redemption of the Firstborn we are removing the energy of the Angel of Death, not only from the firstborn, but from those who participate in the connection. The *Pidyon haBen* establishes the concept that we can remove the energy of death before it becomes manifest in our lives.

However, this precept was not given to the *erev rav* (the anti-kabbalists) because God was angry with them or punishing them but because it will not work for them or on them. This is to teach us the most important lesson, that everything to do with improving our lives cannot become manifested if there is envy, jealousy or hatred; such feelings are all negative energies that are directed outside of ourselves. Consider this, if I have envy, it is not of course directed at myself. It is the envy of someone else that is directed at me. And likewise if I have hatred it is not for myself. I do not have hatred for my finger—I hate someone else. When we fall into these limiting emotions, the idea of improving our lives and everything that pertains to our relationships with others will not work, no matter what we learn or how much we practice.

This is a very revealing section. At first I thought the Ari was angry at the anti-kabbalists. But that made no sense—the Ari would travel miles not to kill an ant. So to say he had ill-will toward evil people is not feasible. The Ari was teaching us that if we want to safeguard ourselves and our families, we must not have hatred, jealousy, or envy in our midst.

Pidyon haBen relates to the Slaying of the Firstborn because we are not referring to the literal firstborn—everything in the Bible is a metaphor. For the kabbalists, even Moses, who is the chariot of the Sefira of Netzach, is a metaphor. We are interested in the life of Moses because his life shows us how the Sefirot of Netzach and Da'at operate, and not for historical purposes.

This portion is a prelude to the next portion of Beshalach, in which we receive the 72 Names of God—the physical demonstration of mind over matter. Before we can apply these Names, we need knowledge; just doing without knowing, without the consciousness of why we are doing, does not work. This is why seven of the Plagues were mentioned in the previous portion of Va'era, and this portion contains the final three Plagues.

The Bible wants to instruct us that the Upper Three Sefirot—Keter, Chochmah, Binah—are considered to be the root. Acting only from the physical world is not enough. To destroy chaos it must be addressed at the level of these Upper Sefirot. Keter, Chochmah, and Binah are code words wherever they appear.

In this portion we understand that if we are going to eliminate chaos, we have to address the cancer, not at the tumor level or when the first cancer cell appears. We must address what brought it about on the immaterial level. This is why these three Sefirot are here, the Keter (seed) of all the chaos, the seed of the plagues was the Slaying of the Firstborn. Why does this plague reign supreme? Why do we refer to the Slaying of the Firstborn as Keter? It is because we are being given an opportunity through this reading about *Pidyon haBen* to remove whatever death might be lurking in our system right now. I would run anywhere in the world to attend a *Pidyon haBen*. We do not know when we may be vulnerable. We may become vulnerable to death energy entering our system because of our negative actions. We, at the Kabbalah Centres, still perform *Pidyon haBen*, even if a man is 80 years old.

Passover and Freedom

We learn about the culmination of Satan in Bo. The Zohar says this culmination is behind all forms of chaos. When we connect with this reading we are able to draw into our lives all that was revealed then and is now available to remove the seed of chaos once again. Not since the time before the sin of Adam were all forms of chaos eradicated. This is what we refer to as the freedom of exodus; where every aspect of every kingdom, whether it be human, animal, mineral, or inanimate, was freed from the bondage of chaos, which is what Passover is really all about.

The final three Plagues appeared in three stages: Binah, Chochmah, and ultimately Keter (which is the Slaying of the Firstborn). As I have mentioned previously, is this death of another human being something we should be merry about? The Slaying of the Firstborn took place on the night of Passover. Should we even be celebrating Passover since it means the death of other people? Why has the corruption of Passover remained for 3,400 years?

We know that slaying of the firstborn did not mean death as it is mentioned in the scripture. In other words, this had nothing to do with Moses or Aaron waving a wand, rod, or staff. No, the Creator Himself performed the slaying of the firstborn, on the night of Passover.

We now know that the Slaying of the Firstborn is a metaphor, and as the Zohar says, if we believe what we read in the Bible that in every household there was a firstborn death, and for this we would celebrate, nothing could be further from the truth. Death, injury or any other form of chaos is not something that could emerge from the Creator, a force of sharing, kindness, mercy, and compassion. We cannot interpret the Creator as One who took pride, as the scripture states, in performing the Slaying of the Firstborn to the extent that He would not give this particular job over to an angel. It is repulsive to think that this is the destruction of the Creator.

Consequently, we understand that what took place is the slaying, the removal of the ultimate seed of chaos that the Satan brings upon, not just human beings, but on the soil and animals.

The purpose of *Pidyon HaBe*n chips away at chaos and mortality, and what happened was that a total chipping away of death became a reality. This has been concealed for 3,400 years. The anti-kabbalists maintained that mortality is the miserable reality of this universe and that immortality is sacrilegious. This corruption persisted despite the fact that this is not what humankind wants to hear, people do not want to experience mortality. It only proves the point that falsehood, pain and suffering are more readily acceptable than truth. Kabbalah presents the truth of this universe.

Unfortunately, the anti-kabbalists have had it their way because, as the Zohar says, they represent the foundation of chaos. These anti-kabbalists are the same *erev rav* (mixed multitude) who, at the revelation of the Torah on Mount Sinai—the physical instrument that drew down the Light to provide the elimination of the root source of Satan and of morality—brought the golden calf that reversed this revelation. The Light does not manifest itself because it is not of a physical nature, so the actual physical Torah Scroll was the necessary instrument that would channel that Lightforce of God to eliminate mortality and all forms of chaos. The anti-kabbalist convinced an entire nation that the golden calf, back then and the computer today (the computer is the modern day golden calf) should replace the Lightforce of God. This corruption is what has been perpetrated as religion for 3,400 years.

Under sometimes unbearable conditions we, at the Kabbalah Centres, have been chipping away at chaos, and have survived, but that does not mean the battle is over. We chip away at a consciousness that mortality is a reality. Unfortunately, even some present at the Kabbalah Centres are still not convinced that immortality is in fact a reality. We ought not place blame on people who do not believe, as there is so much evidence to indicate that pain and suffering are in fact a reality, whether it results in death or not. We owe a debt of gratitude to the pioneer who started all of this, who had the guts to stand up against 3,400 years of tradition. Rav Ashlag, despite unbearable conditions, sometimes physical, social, and mental abuse, made the effort of resistance and selflessness some 80 years ago.

Tefilin Also Wear Away at Death

There is another focal point in this portion, something seemingly insignificant that is explained in the Zohar in reference to this section: *Tefilin* (Phylacteries). *Tefilin* were established as a vital element that deals with the removal of the aspect of death. This does not apply to women; for them it is not required because they have inbuilt protections.

The *Tefilin* are specifically constructed, and what is contained in them, which will be read in this portion in the Torah Scroll, did not come from the imagination of a rabbi. *Tefilin* are another tool to chip away the aspect of death, where the ultimate chaos (pain and suffering) comes to a final end.

Tefilin are so important because they correspond to and relate to the aspect of removing a different part of chaos each and every single day. The sections from the Torah Scroll that are included in these boxes come from the portion of Bo, and help to whittle away at chaos of all forms from our lives, and thus it is required. Every seven years, we must get the *Tefilin* scrolls checked because, as a kabbalist told us, the life span of ink on a parchment is seven years, after which there could be deterioration. These sages knew that the elements could be eating away at the parchment. If this is not our perspective, then it simply is something of a religious nature as presented to the masses for 3,400 years—and then it becomes very insignificant.

All the major tools that create the benefits we derive from the Kabbalah Centres have been scientifically established. But nevertheless the anti-kabbalists say it is one of my gimmicks to make more money so I can buy more cars and castles around the world. This is not a joke, it is a fact. This is what they say the Kabbalah Water is all about. They still persist and people still believe it. This has not deterred us, nor will it ever deter us. But what I experience in no way compares to the abuse of my teacher, Rav Brandwein and my teacher's teacher, Rav Ashlag. These men underwent a deprivation that one could never imagine a human being could inflict on another, physically, socially, and emotionally. By comparison, we are all on easy street; we can make our own choices.

BOOK OF SHEMOT:

Portion of Beshalach

PORTION OF BESHALACH

Beshalach is the Origin and Body of the Zohar

The portion of Beshalach contains the Splitting of the Red Sea, the revelation of the 72 Names of God, and is the origin and body of the Zohar. As stated previously, Egypt was a metaphor for our own chaos, and without the Zohar's explanation about the 72 Names of God, and the connections on Passover, we would have no chance of eliminating chaos in our lives. We need to stop getting upset at others for all the "right" reasons, and allowing a separation to happen, again for all the right reasons.

In this portion we are considering every aspect of chaos—how it operates and how it presents itself to us so we succumb to its logic. We fall prey to it by our choice of the path that will probably lead us to disaster, instead of choosing the path that can bring us happiness, well-being and joy. We also have the story of the Splitting of the Red Sea, which was accomplished by the Israelites themselves, not by God.

The rule of Kabbalah is always the idea of paradox. And we see it here in this portion with its many distortions and contradictions: the Splitting of the Red Sea; the conversations between Moses and the Israelites about wanting to return to Egypt rather than dying in the desert; and Pharaoh suddenly waking up to the true reality that he had made a terrible mistake—all of this makes it abundantly clear that this section contains the greatest dissemination and revelation of a technology that we can soon hopefully utilize to ultimately remove all of the chaos, pain and suffering that surround us, squeezing us into circumstances that seem to be hopeless and from which we could otherwise probably never extricate ourselves.

As I have said in the past, and as science has absolutely confirmed, the mind does control our reality however contradictory this is to the manifested state of chaos. The mind can heal the body, yet, for the most part, hospitals are still filled and people are still going through one trauma after another, with an endless array of future chaos ahead of them. So we have to question if the mind really has dominion over physical reality because it seems that everything we confront in this physical reality leads us to the opposite conclusion. The reason mind over matter has not been successful is that we have not had the ability to connect the mind—which is something so immaterial and non-physical—to the physical reality. Mind over matter is outside the realm of the physical reality.

Yet how do we bring these two sometimes opposite forces together so that the mind can control the physical reality? This is what the portion of Beshalach is all about. Chaos manifests itself only on the level of physical reality—whether it is in the form of cancer, bankruptcy or some kind of social upheaval in one's life. Chaos involves people, money or something else physical. We are taught by the kabbalists that the reason this story appears in such contradictory terms, seemingly making no sense, is to make us aware and expand our consciousness to the understanding that stories in the Bible are a concealment to reveal high-tech knowledge that has yet to be discovered by science. This then is 30th century science. But the Zohar says we do not have to wait until the 30th century because it can be done now. The reason this section is so powerful is because it provides all of humanity with the total application to once and for all rid our lives and this world of all chaos, pain, and suffering.

We have this power; it is our given birthright. However, for the last 3,400 years, the anti-kabbalists, for reasons we have already explained, have aggressively convinced us that the Bible should only be interpreted on a superficial level. This is why the Zohar has been concealed for 2,000 years, and removed from the mainstream of humanity. The goal of the anti-kabbalists is to bring into fruition and reality the goals and ambitions of the Satan. Yes, there are people who are negative for no other reason than to simply be negative. These anti-kabbalists have appeared in every generation, including the present one. However, this was prior to an understanding of the Zohar, which was translated by the founder of The Kabbalah Centre, Rav Ashlag, at the beginning of the last century. So we now have an opportunity to change everything. We now understand that the entire Torah is simply a compendium of spiritual technology that can and will eliminate all of the chaos that, unfortunately, we still have to undergo.

Shemot 13:17 And it was when Pharaoh let the people go, God did not lead them toward the sea on the road through the Philistine country, though that was shorter. For God said, "If they face war, they might change their minds and return to Egypt." 18 So God led the people around by the desert road toward the Red Sea. The Israelites went up out of Egypt armed for battle.

The Consciousness of Miracles

There are many secrets in the first verse of Beshalach. The bible tells us that when Pharaoh sent the nation of Israel out, God did not lead them by the shortest path to the Promised Land because it was too close to the Philistines and God feared that when they would see war or experience difficulty the Israelites would want to return to Egypt. What is scripture talking about? Almost in the same instant that the Israelites left Egypt, God was worried they might want to go back, so He took them around by another way, making matters a little more complicated. This defies logic and it is not true. I believe none of us want to go back to the place that has brought us chaos, pain, and suffering.

It is very strange that a nation that had just witnessed the miracle of Ten Plagues was spared and shielded from experiencing the catastrophic results that the Egyptians endured, and who, at the first sign of difficulty, began complaining to Moses that they wanted to return to Egypt.

Remember they were traveling with a pillar of cloud by day and a fiery ball by night. It was so evident that God's presence was there to protect and defend the Israelites on their journey every day, and without hesitation too. The cloud never left until the fiery ball emerged to lead them forward. In other words, God did not permit one moment of doubt to settle in amongst the people. Do we need scripture to tell us the cloud would not leave until the fiery ball arrived? Yes, we do, says the Zohar because in that one second, our consciousness will change until such a time as we all understand that we have uncertainty. As the scientists say about their own uncertainty principle, this uncertainty exists in all of us.

At the Kabbalah Centres we do not subscribe to this idea because we know we cannot make it with uncertainty. For a little while everything can seem well. The Satan likes to see a big fall far more than he does the little ones. He can wait many years to see the big fall. Sometimes he will even leave us alone until we are 90 years old, and let things seem like they are perfect. But when the Satan is in control things can go bad in a minute. He will catch each of us at the moment he feels it is appropriate.

This is a lesson for us about consciousness; this is the secret of whether we fail or whether, instead, we enjoy miracles every day. If we have not experienced a miracle every day, we have a loss of consciousness and should go back and study the Kabbalah Level One course again because we have forgotten the basic principles of how, why, and on what this technology is based. I do not mean here the miracles we pray for in the daily spiritual connections, where we thank God for those miracles of which we were not aware. This is the rule. Each and every day we should be aware and hear about miracles that actually happen.

Achieving the Splitting of the Red Sea

These Israelites must be very brave people. Is it not sufficient that they saw all of the plagues, and they went out from Egypt? Why are we told right at the beginning of this portion that the Lord feared they would want to go back, so He led them by the way of the Red Sea?

We will go to the Zohar for clarity here:

> "And God led the people about, through the way of the wilderness of the Sea of Reeds," NAMELY, to make way of His place IN ORDER TO EVENTUALLY SPLIT THE SEA OF REEDS. IF NOT FOR THIS, IT WOULD HAVE BEEN ENOUGH TO SIMPLY LEAD THEM THROUGH THE WILDERNESS, AND NOT BY WAY
> —Zohar, Beshalach 3:30

From this passage in the Zohar, we see that God's ultimate objective was to prepare a way of achieving the right place to succeed in the Splitting of the Red Sea, and not as suggested by the Bible. The Zohar seems to contradict the literal translation of the Bible, which says that God did not want to lead them by way of the land of the Philistines because it was too close to Egypt, and God felt that maybe they would relent and decide the whole thing was a mistake—that they should never have gone out of Egypt in the first place. But we know the Zohar does not contradict what is written in the Bible. In fact, the Zohar makes understanding the Bible a little easier since there is so much corruption in translations of the biblical verses. To understand what the verse wants to tell us, we once again turn to the Zohar:

> Rav Yehuda said: "Why the difference? When Israel were in Egypt, it is written, 'Let My people go;' (Shemot 5:1) 'if you refuse to let My people go;' (Shemot 10:4) and, 'Israel is My son, my first born.' (Shemot 4:22) They were not circumcised at that time and were not bound TO THE HOLY ONE, BLESSED BE HE, properly. But once they

were circumcised, had offered the Passover sacrifice, and were bound to Him, He calls them 'the people' and not 'My people.'"

HE ANSWERS, "It was due to the mixed multitude that attached themselves to them and were mixed with them that He calls them 'the people' AND NOT 'MY PEOPLE.'" It is written, "And the Lord plagued the people for the calf they made;" (Shemot 32:35) "the people gathered themselves together to Aaron;" and, "the people saw that Moses delayed." (Ibid. 1) DURING A PERIOD WHEN THE CHILDREN OF ISRAEL WERE IN A DECADENT STATE, HE CALLS THEM SIMPLY, "THE PEOPLE" AND NOT "MY PEOPLE."
—Zohar, Beshalach 3:30-31

We have learned that it was not only the Israelites who left Egypt at that time. In fact the translation of Shemot 13:18 says, "The Israelites went up out of Egypt *armed* for battle." However, the Hebrew word *vachamushim* does not mean "armed;" which is a corruption. The Zohar and other commentators explain that *vachamushim* means that only a fifth of the people who left Egypt were Israelites. In other words, not that four-fifths of the Israelites die but that of all the people who left Egypt, only one fifth were Israelites—the rest were the *erev rav* (mixed multitude)—people who, when they saw the miracles, realized that the god of Egypt was no god at all, and therefore, that there must be another power in the world. When Moses said *ha'am* (that nation) he was not referring to the Israelites but to the people who converted and became the *erev rav* (mixed multitude).

According to Rav Isaac Luria (the Ari), in his volume *Sha'ar haGilgulim* ("Gate of Reincarnations"), those Israelites who were of the Generation of the Exodus are the souls who are now coming back in our generation. This would then mean that most of the Jews today are from the *erev rav*.

There is a dialogue here between Moses and the Lord. The Lord said, "Don't take them." Moses said, "I've got to." Little did Moses know that by taking them this would be the downfall of the Generation of the Exodus. With the incident of the golden calf, the *erev rav* cancelled the gift of immortality that had just been attained through the giving of the Ten Utterances at Mount Sinai. The Ari says the *erev rav* are Jews with the highest intensity of Desire to Receive. The Desire to Receive for the Self Alone represents those people filled with hatred for absolutely no reason, which is the lowest degree of the Desire to Receive. When I say the lowest degree, it is of course at the same time possessed of the highest potential because whatsoever is extremely bad has the potential of a greater conversion. The reason these *erev rav* wanted to convert was because they had an inner drive—their souls were those of Israelites.

God knew these people were the kind of hatred-for-no-reason people we encounter every day. But Moses, on the other hand, said, "I want to speed up the process a little. I know these people can ultimately make their *tikkun* (spiritual correction)." God's reply was, "Look, don't rush it. Go slow. Let them make a couple of corrections—*tikkunim*—as non-Israelites, so that they may purify themselves. This way, when they finally turn into Jewish bodies, the difficulty will not be so bad because their Desire to Receive will not be one of *erev rav*." These were the people who were referred to as *ha'am* (that nation). These were the people who the Bible says God thought were going to return to Egypt because, being the epitome of Desire to Receive for Oneself Alone, God knew that the minute it got a little hot they would abandon everything. They were purely and totally into one aspect: what was comfortable and best for themselves. When they saw Egypt sink, the best thing was to go with the winner—and that is all it was. There was no other reason, and this is why they are called *erev rav*. This answer of the Zohar explains away the paradox of the Bible—that the Israelites wanted to return to Egypt.

It was necessary for the nation that they go through the aspect of the Splitting of the Red Sea. This was to be the miracle that would finally put an end to the Middle Kingdom of Egypt because this was where all of the Egyptian heads of state perished.

Why was the Splitting of the Red Sea so important? The Zohar says this journey to the Splitting of the Red Sea was not for the purpose of performing another miracle but rather it was an essential factor in the destiny of the Israelites.

19 Moses took the bones of Joseph with him because Joseph had made the sons of Israel swear an oath. He had said, "God will surely come to your aid, and then you must carry my bones up with you from this place." 20 After leaving Succoth they camped at Etham on the edge of the desert. 21 By day the Lord went ahead of them in a pillar of cloud to guide them on their way and by night in a pillar of fire to give them light, so that they could travel by day and night. 22 Neither the pillar of cloud by day nor the pillar of fire by night left its place in front of the people.

Shemot 14:1 Then the Lord said to Moses, 2 "Tell the Israelites to turn back and encamp near Pi Hahiroth, between Migdol and the sea. They are to encamp by the sea, directly opposite Baal Zephon. 3 Pharaoh will think, 'The Israelites are wandering around the land in confusion, hemmed in by the desert.' 4 And I will strengthen Pharaoh's heart, and he will pursue them. But I will gain glory for myself through Pharaoh and all his army, and the Egyptians will know that I am the Lord." So the Israelites did this.

The Purpose of Beshalach

The consciousness of the human being has not changed. Moses took the children of Israel by the long route away from Egypt rather than by the direct route because he was afraid they would go back to Egypt. The Israelites did not want to leave Egypt because they did not understand that Egypt was a metaphor for chaos. They wanted to hold onto their chaos, just like we hold onto our chaos today. For 3,400 years, we continue to think this way. We still do not get it. We do not understand what a Kabbalah Centre really is, and we do not take advantage of all it has to offer us. Just like the Israelites did not take advantage of what they knew. We forget like the Israelites in the wilderness forgot. There was a pillar of cloud leading them and a pillar of fire behind them, protecting them. How *could* they forget?

The reason we cannot be rid of chaos, and the reason the Israelites were not able to keep chaos away, is because people cannot keep their certainty. This is the power of Satan. Certainty and chaos cannot co-exist, and if we could keep our certainty we would not fall into chaos.

The portion of Beshalach contains all of the technology that we enjoy today—technology that was the work of Rav Ashlag and Rav Brandwein (original founders of the Kabbalah Centre). Today, the work is ours to use. Thanks to these teachings, we have the knowledge to control our environment and the chaos that life in the physical world inevitably brings. We can bring together so many of our lifetimes to create the *tikkunim*—spiritual corrections—and thus we speed up the process. This process would have brought us despair, disappointment, and frustration if we did not have the technology of the portion of Beshalach. All the teachings of Kabbalah bring us back to the root, which is why we at the Kabbalah Centres spoke about stem cells long before medical science did.

The corruption and concealment of the truth (which began 3,400 years ago)—that all the cosmic events like Rosh Hashanah, Pesach, and so forth, are only for the Jews—has been exposed in our day. We know that the receiving of the Torah on Mount Sinai was for all people in the world. There is no source that contradicts this, not even the Talmud, and of course not the Zohar. This means that if a Christian or Moslem is not given the opportunity to observe Rosh Hashanah he or she has something to be angry about. They, too, were given the technology to change their destiny and remove the chaos that comes each and every single year.

5 When the King of Egypt was told that the people had fled, Pharaoh and his officials changed their minds about them and said, "What have we done? We have sent away the Israelites from serving us!" 6 So he had his chariot made ready and took his people with him. 7 He took six hundred of the best chariots, along with all the other chariots of Egypt, with officers over all of them. 8 The Lord hardened the heart of Pharaoh, king of Egypt, so that he pursued the Israelites, who were marching out with a strong hand. 9 The Egyptians pursued the Israelites and overtook them as they camped by the sea—all Pharaoh's horses and chariots, horsemen and troops—near Pi Hahiroth, opposite Baal Zephon.

The Spiritual Journey is a Struggle Every Day

In these few verses we have the success or failure in our pursuit of happiness, in the pursuit of creating miracles in our lives. Here we are discussing immaterial things that affect our lives and our consciousness.

God told Moses not to take the Israelites by way of the Philistines, so that the Israelites would not lose their consciousness. Many of us who have embarked on this new journey—the journey of delving into and learning the wisdom of Kabbalah—have also begun to realize that this new experience is not a bed of roses. Before the revelation of the tools, scripture warns us to remember that just because we are on this journey there is no guarantee we will be successful. It is a constant struggle each and every single day.

This is why we call the place where we make our connections and listen to the reading of the Torah Scroll a War Room, and not a synagogue. We are here to reinforce ourselves and our consciousness so that we can face the battle all day, every day. Sometimes we *seem* to have a respite from the struggle. Maybe the Satan went to Acapulco on vacation? Do not worry; he will be back. These moments of respite in between bouts of chaos do not mean we have won the war because this war is constant. The higher we elevate and experience more joy, more physical pleasure, whether it is with food or simply energy, the stronger the Satan gets.

In Shemot 13:17, the Bible says that God was afraid the Israelites would want to go back to Egypt. How many times have you heard me say that some people just love to hug their chaos, and they do not want to let go because it is all so familiar to them? All of us have experienced this, where we want to share what we receive from a Kabbalah Centre, and people's response to this is just: "Maybe it is good for you but I'm satisfied with what I've got." Nobody is satisfied, especially if you live in Los Angeles, where denial is the norm. When we first arrived in California in 1980, it was strange to meet people whose children were in institutions or on drugs—and yet these people still said that "things couldn't be better." What were they talking about? There was so much chaos in their lives.

Scripture here teaches us about our tendency to hug our chaos. We could try to rationalize that it is because the chaos is more familiar, and that miracles are a wonderful thing, but they are also new ground. At the Kabbalah Centres we are entering new territory, territory that has been inaccessible and obstructed for 3,400 years. I am not speaking about physical territory but rather the arena of achieving miracles in our lives. Most people think they have control in their lives. This is the familiar road we have taken, not only in this lifetime but possibly in prior lifetimes. This consciousness of uncertainty from prior lifetimes is here with us today, and it is not easy to transform, remove or heal it—and thus, every day is a constant struggle.

This is part of the journey. We are at a Kabbalah Centre to strengthen our certainty, even though everyone and everything is against the conviction that certainty exists. We are facing a battle day in and day out because most people are convinced of the scientific Uncertainty Principle. We will never be rid of this energy force known as the Uncertainty Principle until there is a critical mass in consciousness. It requires everyone's consciousness to achieve certainty. Whatever the case may be, we are faced with the critical impediment of doubt.

We believe that things are under control when something good happens; we may have just witnessed a great miracle and think that now we can lay down our arms—but this is not the case. Remember that with the plague of the Slaying of the Firstborn, which we explained in the previous portion, it was not God out there killing people, it was instead the Keter of the Satan that was destroyed— we removed the seed. However, this was not by virtue of the efforts of the Israelites—that battle was fought by the Lightforce.

Despite the fact that potentially we had removed the Satan from the arena with the Slaying of the Firstborn, we are not discussing physicality here. God hardened the heart of Pharaoh, so that after every great miracle the Israelites could recognize that they were now in control. God made it certain that He laid the Satan down and the Satan pretended he was dead. But the Satan (meaning those negative forces) will continue to awaken until such a time when he will be permanently swallowed up. If we feel we do not have to share anymore, that we do not have to treat every single human being with human dignity, then the Satan is ready again to do battle every day, despite our victories. Those victories are not permanent until such a time as either the critical mass appears or everyone comes to this realization.

Light and Darkness

The most powerful tools, and consequently the most powerful corruption, are found in this portion. In the portion of Bo, Pharaoh drove the Israelites out of Egypt. Then a few sentences later it said that when he was informed they had left, Pharaoh suddenly had second thoughts about sending the Israelites out of Egypt. I have never understood this simple story, with Pharaoh chasing after the Israelites. Why would he chase them? Did he not see the manner by which they destroyed his land? Everything was decimated—the crops, the cities and their flocks. Only the Israelites had livestock remaining. Pharaoh and the Israelites are metaphors. The Zohar says that Pharaoh did not understand what the Israelites were. Not until they left did he comprehend, because he felt the lack of their presence. Darkness cannot co-exist with Light.

When Pharaoh wanted to pursue the Israelites, was it because he was a fool? No, Pharaoh was only acting out the game of Satan. We are armchair detectives here; we think, "Had I not done this and that, everything would have been perfect." We like to think we are brilliant. This is the way of Satan, and we are constantly in his game. Satan provides us with the means to continue within our chaos. He validates anything and everything, no matter how foolish it might be. Satan tells us how clever we are, how that last disaster we caused could have been averted if we had just changed one little thing or not done it a certain way.

This was like Pharaoh. Suddenly he was brilliant. How many times has our own conscience or someone told us not to do something but we think we know better? Because we live in a reactive way, we do not exercise restriction. Too often, we do not make a connection with the technology of the principle of restriction that can beat Satan at his own game. It is the only strategy we have left—everything else plays right into his hands. Without restriction there is no way that these incredible tools we have in Kabbalah can truly be of any use.

10 As Pharaoh approached, the Israelites raised their eyes upwards, and there were the Egyptians, marching after them. They were terrified and cried out to the Lord. 11 They said to Moses, "Was it because there were no graves in Egypt that you brought us to the desert to die? What have you done to us by bringing us out of Egypt? 12 Did we not say to you in Egypt, 'Leave us alone; let us serve the Egyptians?' It would have been better for us to serve the Egyptians than to die in the desert!" 13 Moses answered the people, "Do not be afraid. Stand firm and see the deliverance the Lord will bring you today. The Egyptians you see today you will never see again. 14 The Lord will fight for you; you need only to be quiet." 15 Then the Lord said to Moses, "Why are you crying out to me? Tell the Israelites and move on." 16 Raise your staff and stretch out your hand over the sea to divide the water so that the Israelites can go through the sea on dry ground. 17 I will harden the hearts of the Egyptians so that they will go in after them. And I will gain glory through Pharaoh and all his army, through his chariots and his horsemen. 18 The Egyptians will know that I am the Lord when I gain glory through Pharaoh, his chariots and his horsemen." 19 And the angel of God, who went before the camp of Israel, removed and went behind them; 20 and it came between the camp of Egypt and the camp of Israel; and there was the cloud and the darkness here, yet gave it light by night there; and

the one came not near the other all the night. 21 And Moses stretched out his hand over the sea; and the Lord caused the sea to go back by a strong east wind all the night, and made the sea dry land, and the waters were divided, 22 and the Israelites went through the sea on dry ground, with a wall of water on their right and on their left.

The Holy Name and the 72 Letters

The Zohar says:

> "But lift up your rod." (Shemot14:16) Lift up your rod, upon which is etched the Holy Name, and stretch your hand to the side of the Holy Name. As soon as the waters see the Holy Name, they will flee from it. Therefore, stretch your hand to one side OF THE ROD, because the other sides of the rod will be necessary for other matters, NAMELY, TO HIT THE ROCK.

> Rav Elazar said: "I see that sometimes this rod is called 'the rod of God [lit. Elohim]' and sometimes it is called 'the rod of Moses.'" Rav Shimon said: "In the Book of Rav Hamnuna Saba (the elder), he says that it is all one, whether it says 'THE ROD of the Holy One, blessed be He' or the 'THE ROD of Moses.' The purpose of this rod is to rekindle the aspect of Gevurah. Therefore, THE VERSE SAYS, 'Stretch out your hand,' WHICH MEANS the left hand, which is at the side of Gevurah."

> Rav Shimon said, "Woe to those who do not see and do not look at the Torah. The Torah calls before them daily but

they do not pay attention. Come and behold: water rises in the world and water emerges from the side of Gevurah. But now the Holy One, blessed be He, wanted to dry up the water. Thus, why DOES THE VERSE SAY, 'And stretch out your hand,' which is the Left hand, NAMELY GEVURAH?"

HE ANSWERS, "Rather, 'lift up your rod,' is to dry up the water, and 'stretch out your hand,' is to return the water, to activate the side of Gevurah and to turn the water on Egypt. Therefore, there are two things here, for it is written, 'Lift up your rod, and stretch out your hand over the sea, and divide it.' ONE ELEMENT IS TO DRY OUT THE WATER, AND THE OTHER IS TO TURN THE WATER OVER EGYPT."

HE ASKS, "HOW WAS IT POSSIBLE TO DRY THE LAND IN THE MIDST OF THE SEA, for there were pits IN IT?" HE ANSWERS, "THE Holy One, blessed be He, performed a miracle within a miracle, as is written, 'And the depths were congealed in the heart of the sea.' (Shemot 15:8) They were walking on the dry ground within the sea. This is what is written, 'And the children of Israel went into the midst of the sea on the dry ground.'" (Shemot 14:22)
—Zohar, Beshalach 9:90-94

Why are we told that Moses had to first raise the rod and then stretch out his hand? Is it not enough to simply say stretch out the rod? Could not the Lord have come down and split the sea so the Israelites could walk through, which would be an equal miracle? What is the purpose of raising the rod, then stretching it out? The Zohar explains that these are codes that accomplish different things: raising the rod was to dry out the water, and then stretching out the hand was to return the waters as they were before—and in this way two things were accomplished. Why was it necessary to do it this way? Here the Zohar teaches us the essence of mind over matter.

In another section of the Zohar we learn that at the time of Creation, God created water with a stipulation: although water has an internal energy-intelligence of Chesed (sharing and expanding), at the time of the Splitting of the Red Sea, water would have to change its natural intrinsic characteristic. In this instance, water would cease stretching out, cease flowing, cease seeking its own level, and instead, water would stop. It was already established at the time of Creation that humankind would control matter, no matter how far-reaching or strong any substance was.

Mind-intelligence travels because of a Holy Name. Why is it holy? If we are religious people, we might say that something holy must have some holy substance to it. From a kabbalistic point of view, though, we know what *kadosh* (holy) means. It is the Three-Column System, a circuit of energy. When we say a cosmic event is holy or similarly when a man is holy, this does not mean a display of religiosity. Rather, it is someone who expresses and shows by their own actions that they operate in a Three-Column System.

This Holy Name (Heb: *Shem haKadosh*) is a vehicle that can handle a circuit of energy. A holy man is simply a channel for the circuit of higher forms of energy-intelligence to flow through. If a person who thinks they are holy says, "It is mine," they involve themselves, and then they are no longer a channel. Holy only means a channel. When Moses used the rod with the Holy Name engraved upon it, he now had the proper channel by which to connect to water. This was the energy-intelligence that reminded the water of the stipulation to stop flowing, which was instated at the time of Creation. The water stopped flowing only because Moses was in a position to be able to communicate to the water using the Holy Name.

Rav Isaac Luria (the Ari) established in his book, Gate of Meditations, that if we want to talk to the cosmos and to an intelligence, we have to use something physical in a certain way, together with the Holy Name. For example, on Shabbat, when we meditate on the twelve loaves of the *challot*, using certain Holy Names, these *challot* permit the connection to wherever we want to go. We must have the Holy Name. If we do not have the Holy Name, according to Kabbalah, we can sit and meditate on a mountain for the rest of our lives but nothing will be achieved.

Moses used the Holy Name and this brought the command, causing the water at that moment to stop flowing. Because physical matter can only handle one command at a time, Moses could not tell the water to both split apart and come back at the same time. This is why he raised the rod and then stretched his hand over the waters.

Immediately following this demonstration of mind over matter, and before the action of the Splitting of the Red Sea actually took place, we have the aspect of the 72 letters in the three verses—Shemot 14:19, 20, 21. Each of these verses begins with a letter *Vav*, and when the three *Vavs* are placed in a particular formation, they form the letter *Bet* (בּ), the letter by which the entire world was created. The Zohar says that one of the reasons the *Bet* was chosen over all the other Hebrew letters is because the Bet has the right qualifications—it is made up of three letter *Vavs*, indicating that it has Three Columns. This letter is where the Three-Column System of Right, Left, and Central comes from. I call it the Super Force because it contains *Kadosh* (Holy)—everything is in threes.

The 72 Names of God are created with three biblical verses, each containing 72 letters. If you have studied even a little Kabbalah, you know the significance of why there must be three. Three is *kadosh*, and three makes up a total system. There must be a Desire to Receive (Left Column); a Desire to Share (Right Column); and a Desire to Restrict (Central Column). The letter *Bet* was chosen because it could be the channel by which all intelligences of the human being, to rule and control everything in the cosmos, could manifest because everything was created with a seed of the Three-Column System.

The Composition of the 72 Names

Vayisa the first word of Shemot 14:19, is connected with the Right Column, says the Zohar.

19.וַיִּסַּע מַלְאַךְ הָאֱלֹהִים, הַהֹלֵךְ לִפְנֵי מַחֲנֵה יִשְׂרָאֵל, וַיֵּלֶךְ,
מֵאַחֲרֵיהֶם; וַיִּסַּע עַמּוּד הֶעָנָן, מִפְּנֵיהֶם, וַיַּעֲמֹד, מֵאַחֲרֵיהֶם

19. And the angel of God, who went before the camp of Israel,
removed and went behind them;

כהת	אכא	ללה	מהש	עלם	סיט	ילי	והו
הקם	הרי	מבה	יזל	ההע	לאו	אלד	הזי
וההו	מלה	ייי	נלך	פהל	לוו	כלי	לאו
ועיר	לכב	אום	ריי	שאה	ירת	האא	נתה
ייז	רהע	וזעם	אני	מנד	כוק	להוו	יוו
מיה	עשל	ערי	סאל	ילה	וול	מיכ	ההה
פוי	מבה	נית	נגא	עמם	הועי	דני	והו
מוזי	ענו	יהה	ומב	מצר	הרח	ייל	נמם
מום	היי	ליבמ	ראה	וזבו	איע	מנק	דמב

223

The first chart is Shemot 14:19, beginning with the word *vayisa*, and it flows forward like water, in an extending manner (top right towards the left). This is our code that establishes the channel for the establishment of the Right Column, the proton. These letters control every particle of the atom. Every form of energy that exists in this Universe is encompassed. By connecting with these letters, we are connecting with all aspects of the Right Column of the atom, which is the proton.

Vayavo, the first word of the second verse, Shemot 14:20, is connected with the Left Column.

> 20. וַיָּבֹא בֵּין מַחֲנֵה מִצְרַיִם, וּבֵין מַחֲנֵה יִשְׂרָאֵל, וַיְהִי הֶעָנָן
> וְהַחֹשֶׁךְ, וַיָּאֶר אֶת-הַלָּיְלָה; וְלֹא-קָרַב זֶה אֶל-זֶה, כָּל-הַלָּיְלָה
>
> 20. and it came between the camp of Egypt and the camp of Israel;
> and there was the cloud and the darkness here, yet gave it light by
> night there; and the one came not near the other all the night.

והו	ילי	סיט	עלם	מהש	ללה	אכא	כהת
הזי	אלד	לאו	ההע	יזל	מבה	הרי	הקם
לאו	כלי	לוו	פהל	נלך	ייי	מלה	חהו
נתה	האא	ירת	שאה	ריי	אום	לכב	ושר
יחו	להח	כוק	מנד	אני	חעם	רהע	ייז
ההה	מיכ	וול	ילה	סאל	ערי	עשל	מיה
והו	דני	החש	עמם	ננא	נית	מבה	פוי
נמם	ייל	הרח	מצר	ומב	יהה	ענו	מחי
דמב	מנק	איע	חבו	ראה	יבמ	היי	מום

The second chart of Shemot 14:20 begins with *vayavo*, and we go in reverse order (bottom left towards the right). Why does the Left Column go in the opposite direction? Those of you who have learned the Study of the Ten Luminous Emanations can understand what must be done with your Desire to Receive from an energy-intelligence point of view. It must be restricted; it must be pushed backwards. And so these letters that control the electron, the negative aspect of the atom, flow in an opposite direction.

And *Vayet*, the first word of Shemot 14:21, manifests the Central Column.

---

21. וַיֵּט מֹשֶׁה אֶת־יָדוֹ, עַל־הַיָּם, וַיּוֹלֶךְ יְהוָה אֶת־הַיָּם בְּרוּחַ
קָדִים עַזָּה כָּל־הַלַּיְלָה, וַיָּשֶׂם אֶת־הַיָּם לֶחָרָבָה; וַיִּבָּקְעוּ, הַמָּיִם.

21. And Moses stretched out his hand over the sea; and the Lord caused the sea to go back by a strong east wind all the night, and made the sea dry land, and the waters were divided.

←

כ·ה·ת	א·כ·א	ל·ל·ה	מ·ה·ש	ע·ל·ם	סי·ט	י·לי	ו·הו
ה·ק·ם	ה·ר·י	מ·ב·ה	י·ז·ל	ה·ה·ע	ל·א·ו	א·ל·ד	ה·ז·י
ו·ה·ו	מ·ל·ה	ייי	נ·ל·ך	פ·ה·ל	ל·ו·ו	כ·ל·י	לא·ו
ו·ע·ר	ל·כ·ב	א·ו·ם	ר·יי	ש·א·ה	י·ר·ת	ה·א·א	נ·ת·ה
ייז	ר·ה·ע	ו·ה·ע·ם	א·נ·י	מ·נ·ד	כ·ו·ק	ל·ה·ו	יו·ו
ב·י·ה	ע·י·ע·ל	ע·ר·י	ס·א·ל	י·ל·ה	ו·ו·ל	מ·י·כ	ה·ה·ה
פ·ו·י	מ·ב·ה	נ·י·ת	נ·ג·א	ע·מ·ם	ה·ו·ש	ד·נ·י	ו·ה·ו
ב·ו·ז·י	ע·נ·ו	י·ה·ה	ו·מ·ב	מ·צ·ר	ה·ר·ו	יי·ל	ג·ם·ם
מ·ו·ם	ה·י·י	י·ב·מ	ר·א·ה	ו·ז·ב	א·י·ע	מ·נ·ק	ד·מ·ב

The final chart, Shemot 14:21—*vayet*, which is the Central Column, runs in the same order (top right towards the left). Now, for the neutron, this is a serious business. We in Kabbalah are precise. Every one of these letters in the third verse controls every particle of the neutron. The physicists, on the other hand, end each scholarly article with something like "this is not conclusive." It was essential for the Israelites to receive this knowledge before the Splitting of the Red Sea because all the ten miracles of the Ten Plagues were not particularly out of the ordinary—even all of the firstborn who died. Death is not a miracle; death is just something that will eventually come.

The Letter Bet

If we can connect with the letter *Bet*, we have connected with the seed of the universe. Connecting with the *Bet* means behaving as a *kadosh*, which is behaving in a manner according to the Three-Column System. Although it seems to be so difficult because we have not been too successful in the past, there is very little needed to become a *kadosh*. All it requires is an aspect of not hating, and making use of the Three-Column System, like in the atom, with its proton (Desire to Share), electron (Desire to Receive) and the neutron (Desire to Restrict). We need all three to create a circuit because without a Desire to Receive there is no aspect of sharing. We cannot share that which we do not have. Nowhere in kabbalistic teachings do we say the Desire to Receive should be done away with—which incidentally is different from Eastern traditions. Within the wisdom of Kabbalah we are stronger and better with the Desire to Receive than without it. However, we have to first bind and control it by sharing and restriction.

The 72 Names of God are the expression of the Lightforce of God, and there is a condition that before we can implement the 72

Names we must be connected with the *Bet*, with the three *Vavs* that form the letter *Bet* (ב). If we are not in tune with the three *Vavs*, forget it—although we may make every attempt to make use of these Names, we cannot.

Moses demonstrated that mind can control matter if we have the proper channels. The channels the Israelites were going to make use of were contained in these three verses. But having the Names and desiring to use them is not sufficient because it is through knowledge that we make the connection. We must know everything there is to know of these 72 Names of God—to the degree that we can understand, of course. This will further increase the intensity of the channel.

The Zohar explains that God brought the Israelites to the Red Sea because it was necessary to make that miracle wherein nature would change its course, and would manifest there on that specific day. Death did not change its course with the Slaying of the Firstborn, who all died at once. Some commentators even want to explain away the Splitting of the Red Sea by natural phenomena—such as that a strong wind came and dried up the sea. It is possible but we are not discussing the Splitting of the Red Sea, which is not significant. This is not what the Bible, in its coded manner, intends for us. Here, for the first time, a channel and a system of how to connect with and control the Super Force of the *Bet* came into existence, became manifest. In other words, the Red Sea was the effect and it was also the manifestation. This system of the 72 Names became established by the Splitting of the Red Sea. The Red Sea was essential so that this knowledge, which was given earlier could become manifest. The Splitting of the Red Sea was not merely to demonstrate a miracle but also to activate the command of mind over matter—and thus became manifest.

The 72 letters are connections with each individual form of energy—whether it be Right Column, Desire to Share; Left Column, Desire to Receive; or Central Column, Restriction—to create a force when it is necessary. For example, on Shabbat we use the Name, *Mem, Hei, Shin*, which is a code for the Three-Column System to be used for healing—*Shabbat Hi Milizok*. Unfortunately, many synagogues are not familiar with the *Mem, Hei, Shin* because it is in code. Woe to those who interpret and translate the Bible literally because it is an exercise in futility. How did we go so wrong? I have to say I think that religion became politics. If we participate in this prayer and are not connecting to the code of *Mem, Hei, Shin*, that prayer of ours probably adds up to zero. This is because the intent of this prayer is to conceal, the same way the soul is concealed in a body. Understanding the meaning of the words is unimportant. It is the electricity, the charge that we put into these same words that produces the effect. Without the electricity, we can have a cable system but nothing happens. The charge in this case is these letters that act as channels for the healing—as we have said, it is a code.

These various 72 Names are referred to as the *Shem haKadosh* (the Holy Name)—and they are not such a mystery. The truth is there for everyone to see. But, as I said before, there is one requirement: Love Thy Neighbor. We can make use of the letters to be in the right place at the right time—and then we have really entered a new era of mind over matter, an era in which we shall control our destiny.

כהת	אכא	ללה	מהש	עלם	סיט	ילי	והו
הקם	הרי	מבה	יזל	ההע	לאו	אלד	הזי
וההו	מלה	ייי	נלך	פהל	לוו	כלי	לאו
ושר	לכב	אום	ריי	שאה	ירת	האא	נתה
ייז	רהע	ועם	אני	מנד	כוק	להו	יוו
מיה	עשל	ערי	סאל	ילה	וול	מיכ	ההה
פוי	מבה	נית	נגא	עמם	הוש	דני	והו
מוזי	ענו	יהה	ומב	מצר	הרוז	ייל	נמם
מום	היי	יבמ	ראה	וזבו	איע	מנק	דמב

You Will Be Silent

In Shemot 14:14 we have that famous verse: *HaShem yilachem lachem ve'atem tacharishun*, "The Lord will fight for you, you need only to be quiet." This means that when it comes down to it, we will stop and we will not waste ourselves on any battles. The Lightforce of God will do it for us while we remain silent. Perhaps someone has wronged us, maybe stolen our entire life savings, our retirement plan—maybe everything has been stolen. In a single moment, our life can shatter into pieces for whatever reason, but we cannot let this get to us. Most of us think we have to get it all back but here God says we must simply be quiet. He is telling us that we have the tools to assist us in such a position, and this is the *Yud, Yud, Lamed*—one of the 72 Names of God for "letting go." This is the way to conduct battles. We do not expend energy on wanting to get it all back.

God says to Moses, "Who are you screaming and yelling at?" Moses is screaming and yelling here because he is telling us to arouse our consciousness.

I will tell you a sorrowful story. The Israelites crossed the Red Sea. All those miracles were great. They sang the *Az Yashir* (Song of the Sea) and said "Let us see what the coming events are about." Everything was great. They then traveled three days in the wilderness, and did not have water. They could not find an oasis in the desert. Then they came to a place, an oasis, but the water was bitter. (Shemot 15:23) And so what did they do? What else but complain?

Amen and Infusing Zeir Anpin into Malchut

In our morning connection we go to war, for the lack of a better expression. There is no question it is a war each and every single day. We do not wait for some unexpected chaos to befall us. A preemptive strike is what we do.

It says the Israelites will come to believe in God and in Moses. The Zohar questions how much must we witness before we become certain that we can accomplish what we set out to do. When faced with imminent death (drowning in the sea or being slain by the Egyptians), had the Israelites not been certain of the knowledge at that moment—that when this physical reality is combined with the Flawless Universe it equals Amen (numerically 91)—they would not have been able to part the sea. The Holy Names of God, *Adonai* (*Alef, Dalet, Nun,* and *Yud* =65) and the Tetragrammaton (*Yud, Hei, Vav,* and *Hei* =26), merged together equal 91, which is, as we have just seen, Amen. Saying Amen is a powerful tool when said with the consciousness to bring Zeir Anpin, the Flawless Universe, into this physical cesspool of Malchut, where we are. Once the Tetragrammaton is infused into this cesspool, all chaos disappears.

If God is merciful, filled with loving kindness, why do we see so much chaos? There is not a day that goes by when we are not confronted with chaos. However, we need to know that it is here today, gone tomorrow. In the back of our minds, never to be forgotten, are the Israelites who, before the Splitting of the Red Sea took place, knew that the withdrawal of the water on both sides would not come from God. Because of the law of Bread of Shame, this miracle could only take place through the effort of the Israelites themselves.

The Israelites saw Pharaoh himself and his entire army in hot pursuit to bring them back to Egypt. With this first moment of difficulty they wished they had never left their bondage. As scripture states, at that moment the Israelites noticed the danger of the sea (Heb. *Yam Suf*) before them. The translation for the words *Yam Suf* in this section is "Red Sea;" *Yam* means "sea," but it is difficult to understand how the word *suf* comes to be translated as "red" because the Hebrew word for "red" is *adom*. The Hebrew word *suf* or *sof* usually means "end." This is another indication that the internal or concealed meaning of the Torah has yet again been corrupted.

The lesson we are being taught here is that if we wish to have control over our own destiny there is no place for doubt. When we apply all of the tools that we have learned from Kabbalah, and they do not seem to work—they have not removed the chaos that we are experiencing at that moment—then our consciousness may not be in full accord with the tools we have been given. The moment we lose this consciousness of certainty—the moment doubts arise—this system ceases to operate for us. It must be emphasized that this system of Kabbalah will not function if we are in a state of doubt. As we read in this portion, it is important to strengthen our conviction that we do indeed have the ability to control the chaotic physical reality.

In all the years that I studied in a Yeshiva, I had not learned that the 72 Names of God were contained in three verses of the biblical portion of Beshalach. It is thanks to Rav Isaac Luria (the Ari Ha Kadosh), that we know this.

In verse 14:10, when the Bible says the children of Israel screamed and yelled to God, this is us. They have the clouds of glory by day and the pillar of fire by night, and yet now they are complaining to Moses, asking "Was it because there were no graves in Egypt that you brought us here to die?" (Shemot 14:11) The moment that tragedy appears imminent we lose all forms of consciousness and are totally consumed by the moment—all of a sudden all is lost. This is what separates the men from the boys or the women from the girls. This is the difference.

What is the purpose and effect of screaming? Screaming awakens; it elevates a dormant consciousness. In moments of imminent danger most people cry out or scream but what is the purpose of screaming? Perhaps it is simply instinct, and we do not know why we do it.

God's response to the pleas of the Israelites was *mah titzak elai* (Why are you screaming at Me?) These three words eliminate the whole purpose of prayer. But to Whom should we pray, if not to God? Is that not what all the houses of worship are about? God's response was, "Jump into the sea."

The Zohar raises the point that with these tools the physical difficulties the Israelites faced at that moment (stuck between Pharaoh and the sea) should have disappeared—and they did.

The sea opened up by the certainty of one man who jumped in. Nachshon Ben Aminadav went into the water, and when it reached his nostrils he continued on further. At that moment, and because of his certainty, the sea split.

Water, as we have learned from the study of Kabbalah, is mercy (Heb: *chesed*). And *chesed* has only one characteristic: to do good. Therefore, we should be capable of living underneath the sea for days or even years. But the ability to live under the sea has been lost. Water is not about causing death. Only because of the original sin— because of the Tree of Knowledge—did the water become corrupt in this way.

The sea was split with the *Ayin-Bet Shemot* (72 Names), meaning the force that polluted and created a condition of drowning became separated from the true nature of the water. The Zohar states that there were civilizations who lived beneath the surface of the water. Whether the Israelites walked along the bottom of the sea with water suspended on either side or whether perhaps the possibility of drowning in deep water was removed, whatever the interpretation, this man—Nachshon Ben Aminadav—knew the risk, yet had the conviction of mind over matter; that the water, the sea could not cause death. Even as the water reached his nostrils, Nachshon was undeterred, still convinced that he had control. He did not know how it would manifest but he knew it would not cause harm.

Why Are You Calling to Me?

I want to stress the importance of this portion and these three words: *mah titzak elai* (Why are you calling to Me?). When the Israelites faced the sea in front of them and the Egyptians behind them, in their minds was certain death. When the fear of dying overtook them, they completely forgot they had total control over the physical domain. Through the Ten Plagues completely unnatural manifestations occurred.

This section has gone largely unnoticed, yet it contains these three words in which God's reply was, essentially, that the Israelites should help themselves. God was telling them that He would bestow upon them the tools by which they could help themselves. If we ever feel like crying out helplessly, it is because we are not exercising what we have learned. There is not one single aspect of the physical reality that cannot be altered by us—and we must remember this. For some of us, if it does not happen immediately, we lose our certainty. It took me 21 years to change what seemed to have been an impossible situation. I persevered for 21 years. Not once did I hesitate, not once did I doubt that it would not come about. We want to get rid of the idea of time. Those 21 years were for me but a day. Do not ask why it is not happening now, or how long it will take. If we are still asking, it will not work for us. These are the questions the Satan puts in our mind. He will give every conceivable reason why it is not working—and there is no such thing because it works.

Science agrees that our consciousness is 99 percent of our reality. So why is it taking so long for us to internalize this fact? Why has it taken 3,400 years to implant this idea, when everyone agrees that our consciousness is all that there is to us? With consciousness and the tools—for our consciousness is nothing without them—we can remove all illusions. If someone says he has been doing everything and it is still not working, then I say there is something missing in their efforts. Perhaps they are not sharing, not treating others with human dignity; invariably, there is something wrong, and there is no excuse. People often ask me why it doesn't happen for them. Miracles happen for everyone, and I have seen miracles, and then more miracles. I remember hearing about the miracle of the revelation of stem cells. For as long as I have been teaching at The

Centre I have repeated what Rav Isaac Luria (the Ari) said 400 years ago: an arm will grow back, a severed foot will return, a damaged heart will heal. It is such a revelation, and science agrees—but science also disagrees. If someone has lost a limb they can still feel it—they still feel pain where the limb once was; and they even scratch that empty space. Altogether they feel it as if it were still there.

The greatest medical discovery in history was announced not long ago—they found stem cells, even in adults. This brings up some other questions though: such as why do the stem cells not enable the growth of a new heart? Every seven years we are a new person; when we reach seven years old we are not the same person we were when we were born—there is a complete transformation. By the age of 14, we have made another complete transformation but after age 21, a problem starts up and we go progressively downhill physically, eventually becoming old. We know that the *Yud, Kaf, Shin* (י.כ.ש) from the Ana Beko'ach can make us young again, and that the *mikveh* (ritual bath) can also make us younger. We do not have to become older. We can rejuvenate the physical body because we know how to activate the stem cells. The Kabbalah Water combined with the *Kedushah* in the prayer of Keter in Musaf of Shabbat, Rosh Chodesh, and the other cosmic events, as well as the Kiddush of the Shabbat Third Meal, all have the power of activating stem cells and strengthening the immune system, rejuvenating and healing the body.

The Revelation of the 72 Names for all Nations

I have not found any other commentary, other than the Zohar, that stops and takes notice of what is happening here. The Zohar says the Splitting of the Sea was not to impress the Israelites, who so far had not even been impressed with the Plagues that happened

in Egypt. They were constant complainers before and after the
Splitting of the Red Sea. It is not intelligent for us to believe that
the *Kriat Yam Suf* was done for any other purpose than to provide
the Israelites with some greater intelligent Force. This alone was
the reason for the Splitting of the Red Sea. It was to reveal the 72
Names of God, which occurred before the waters divided. The 72
Names is the secret by which the Israelites were going to control
this universe.

It is said the road to hell is paved with good intentions, so
intentions are never sufficient. What is necessary is the
manifestation of thoughts and the manifestation of meditations.
The reason the Israelites proceeded to split the Red Sea was so they
could come to manifest the awesome energy of the 72 Names and
break the totality of the power of the Egyptians. The splitting of the
sea was only an effect of the 72 Names. It was only then that the
72 Names became manifest by the nation of Israel in this World of
Asiyah (the World of Action). Until this time, the 72 Names existed
only for Abraham, Isaac, and Jacob, and the rest of the Chariots.
But all the Israelites individually and collectively, or for that matter
any nation, had never experienced the opportunity to express
these 72 Names until this point. Only now were these Names
able to become part of the cosmos, and thus become part of our
universal intelligence.

These Names could only become manifest on the Seventh Day of
Passover. In other words, we do not celebrate the Seventh Day of
Pesach because the miracle of the Splitting of the Red Sea happened
on that day. We celebrate this day as a cosmic event because this is
the day the power of the 72 Names became manifest in our physical
reality. The Zohar says that God's purpose in sending the Israelites
in the direction He did was to establish this kind of power.

Erev Rav and the Downfall of the Generation

The *erev rav* were part of this group that captured the intelligence of the 72 Names, and believed that now there was nothing they had to fear. Whatever they wanted, whatever they thought of, whatever they did, they felt they were in control. However, they never really connected with the Names. This enormous power that they acquired brought with it the downfall of the Generation of the Exodus. They never made it; they all died in the wilderness because this power brought them to a level of furthering their own egotistical, selfish desires, and this brought their downfall.

Therefore, there was a decree banning the study of the Zohar, except by a select few, until about 250 years ago, when Rav Avraham Azulai openly declared, in the introduction to his book, *Sefer Or haChama* ("Light of the Sun") that the decree was no longer in force. We are in the Age of Aquarius, and now the Zohar and Kabbalah are available to anyone who wishes to study this wisdom. The chart of the 72 Names of God, as we know it today, was not included in early editions of the Zohar. I was not the first one to publish the 72 Names of God in the Zohar. It was Rav Ashlag in his translation and commentary (The Sulam) who felt the time had come when anyone who wished to go into a bookstore and purchase the Zohar could do so, and with it have the opportunity of studying this awesome power of the 72 Names of God.

Accordingly, the three verses of Shemot 14:19, 20, 21 each contain 72 letters—and not by chance. These three verses are essential to establishing the Splitting of the Red Sea. But if we look at what happened before the miracle, the manifestation of these Names, and see what happened after the miracle, we notice that the Israelites did not change. So what was the purpose of a miracle when it had absolutely no effect on the Israelites at that time? In fact, have we today observed the miracle of the Splitting of the Red Sea? No. So of what significance is it to those of us who observe, in accordance with the Torah, the Seventh Day of Passover as a holiday? What does it do for us?

The Zohar says the Seventh Day of Pesach (Passover) is a time when we can connect to the manifestation of the 72 Names of God. But what about those who might take this chart of the 72 Names of God and use it for wrongdoing? Rav Avraham Azulai assures us that because this is a metaphysical system it cannot be fooled with. We cannot fool intelligences. We can maybe pretend we are someone else other than who we are on a physical level but when we begin to involve ourselves with an energy-intelligence level, there is no fooling anyone. We are told by Rav Avraham Azulai, and most of the ancient sages, that there are prerequisites before we can make use of the 72 Names of God. This does not mean praying three times a day or keeping the Sabbath. The prerequisite is to "love your neighbor as yourself." If someone is part of the *erev rav*—the epitome of hatred for no reason—they will be afraid. The *erev rav*, at the time of the exodus, were the ones who constantly complained to Moses and wanted to return to the safety of Egypt. These people were not able to capture the power of the 72 Names of God. They had been handed the power to control the universe but they could not connect with it. They had the total knowledge. They were there at the same time as everyone else but they could not make use of this knowledge because there are certain spiritual prerequisites to permit making use of these 72 Names.

72 Names and the Power of Restriction

The technology of the 72 Names of God has its origins in the portion of Beshalach. In all my years of rabbinical studies I never knew that there are three verses in this portion that contain 72 letters each, and even if I had known I never would have understood their significance. The Zohar reveals that three verses in this portion contain 72 letters each and, when combined in certain configurations, they become a potent tool to make things possible.

We are getting closer to a critical mass of consciousness; miracles are happening that The Kabbalah Centres are involved with, and which are directly related to the 72 Names of God. Peace, tranquility, and fulfillment will not come to human civilization without the concern and the efforts of the masses. No one individual, not even Moses himself, could bring an end to Satan or chaos alone. Each individual *contributes* to that which is necessary to create miracles in his or her life. If we achieve miracles, it is because of the effort of thousands of people who are making use of the certainty principle and the kabbalistic tools that are now available to the masses—so we all may enjoy this gift of God.

These three verses were concealed until the Zohar revealed the secrets contained within them. The entire world can benefit from their emergence today. The 72 Names of God are the most powerful tool, more powerful than physical weaponry, and they are at our disposal to bring an end to war, bloodshed, chaos, pain, and suffering. There is so much concealed in this section, and therefore so much is revealed, to the highest level.

What we notice from these three verses—Shemot 14:19, 20, and 21—is that there are three letters that together total a combination of one important powerful collection of letters. Today, we know that the number three symbolizes Right (Desire to Share), Left (Desire to Receive), and Central Column (Desire to Receive for the Sake of Sharing).

We have only learned about restriction in the past 35 years; I had never heard this word before Kabbalah. What does restriction mean? **Restriction is the very foundation of all this technology,**

and it means not to become reactive. There is no way that we can constantly be within a consciousness of being like God—being proactive—unless we step back. If someone slaps me in the face, I should stop for a moment and think about it. I may decide to slap them back but, at that moment, I restrict. This is the foundation of how we become like God—like the Light.

Without restriction we can be in command of all the technology that will ever become available—have it literally in the palm of our hands—and yet it will not work for us. When people claim that they are using the tools, yet they do not work, it is because of those times when the opportunity arose but they did not exercise the principle of restriction. We must say to ourselves that we will not react to the news, to events, circumstances or whatever misfortune is suddenly thrust upon us. If we say, no, we do not accept it as such, and move back, then all this technology will and does work for us—but it will not work without this consciousness of restriction.

I always recommend that no matter how long one has been studying Kabbalah, one should regularly take the Power of Kabbalah Level One course again because, as I have heard time and again, with people who have studied it all, and know it all, restriction is still not always being implemented as part of their individual consciousness. We are no longer like God when we are reactive. These tools to be proactive are meant to be in the hands of those following the path of the Lightforce of God. We can never achieve a proactive state of consciousness if we do not exercise restriction on every step of the way—especially for those of us who are weak at times and succumb to the game of Satan, as is so clearly demonstrated in this portion.

The mind can heal the body; it is consciousness that directs every movement of our hand. The hand does not make its own decision. The bridge has been lost for 3,400 years. Now we want to reestablish this bridge between consciousness—an immaterial, non-physical entity—with that which is physical. There is only one answer regarding how to bridge the two—and it is with the 72 Names of God. There is no other answer. Scientists can be convinced, and talk about mind over matter, but they will never achieve that kind of result without employing the 72 Names.

Today, without the ability of restriction to remove a reactive state of consciousness, freedom can never be achieved. You can make your own rules if you want but if you want to play in the game of removing chaos, these are the rules. This is why there are three letters in each of the 72 Names of God on the chart: Right, Left and Central. We have this opportunity to have the consciousness that we want to tap into, and it does not require extra hours at the office for 40 years. With the reading of this portion, we have an opportunity to tap into the energy of Central Column, and, in the immediate future too, wondrous miracles will await us.

The Greatest Story Ever Told

We have come to understand the importance of this portion's influence, which is the infusion of the greatest story ever told, a miracle of God that comes once in a lifetime, once in a millennium. And I am not referring to the Splitting of the Red Sea, which has never been duplicated.

In this section, humankind was once again empowered, as it had not been since the fall of Adam, with the possibility of controlling our destiny, controlling our environment and, more importantly, controlling the removal of chaos from our lives.

The Red Sea incident is about the manifestation of mind over matter through the 72 Names of God. As we all know, and we speak about this so often, the removal of any form of chaos, of cancer, for example, is not going to come about by the incision of a knife and the removal of a tumor. Never. It has got to all disappear. But how does something disappear? It is against the basic principles of physics.

Matter can change forms but it never disappears. What we can accomplish with the 72 Names is the conversion of chaos into joy. It is not about just hiding the chaos or removing it and placing it elsewhere. **Negativity must be reversed; it has to be restored to a constructive positive level of consciousness because there is nothing but consciousness.** When we speak of the 72 Names, we are talking about achieving a direct communion with this power. This can only come to us on Shabbat, which has nothing to do with the idea of rest. Taking advantage of the tools, and of the information we have access to, can bring about a better life. Getting rid of the darkness cannot come about simply by cutting it out and moving it elsewhere. We have the great advantage on Shabbat of the full impact of the power of the 72 Names. We must realize that there is no more powerful force in this universe than our mind, our consciousness, and by the same token having a certainty that we can make things happen, that we can change things, as we have done. We can change the course of history. For 3,400 years, people were ignorant of this but we have brought this empowerment to tens of millions of people of all persuasions around the world over the past many years.

How do we do something like this? On a physical level, we do not have the resources. But in the mind, we ourselves can reach everything and everyone. With the power of the Lightforce of God, we have the capacity to change everything of a physical nature.

22 And the Israelites went through the sea on dry ground, with a wall of water on their right and on their left. 23 The Egyptians pursued them, and all Pharaoh's horses and chariots and horsemen followed them into the sea. 24 During the last watch of the night the Lord looked down from the pillar of fire and cloud and confused the Egyptian army. 25 He made the wheels of their chariots come off so that they had difficulty driving. And the Egyptians said, "Let us get away from the Israelites! The Lord is fighting for them against Egypt." 26 Then the Lord said to Moses, "Stretch out your hand over the sea so that the waters may flow back over the Egyptians and their chariots and horsemen." 27 Moses stretched out his hand over the sea, and at daybreak the sea went back to its place. The Egyptians were fleeing toward it, and the Lord tossed them in the sea. 28 The water flowed back and covered the chariots and horsemen—the entire army of Pharaoh that had followed the Israelites into the sea. Not one of them survived. 29 But the Israelites went through the sea on dry ground, with a wall of water on their right and on their left. 30 That day the Lord saved Israel from the hands of the Egyptians, and Israel saw the Egyptians lying dead on the shore. 31 And when the Israelites saw the Great Hand of the Lord displayed against the Egyptians, the people feared the Lord and put their trust in Him and in Moses His servant.

Negativity Affects the Entire Universe

We read about that most historic of events in the human story, the Splitting of the Red Sea, which the sages explain is not an event solely for us. The Zohar explains this event, and repeatedly asks if we think God up there is happy when He sees misery. Do we think He was happy when He saw the Egyptians drowning? This negativity of the Egyptians drowning affects everything—the trees, the mountains, animals, everything in our environment—and it also affects all of us, each and every human being. So we should not be happy at the suffering of others, since every form of negativity affects this entire universe. Negativity has an influence and creates pollution of many kinds.

So with regard to this event of the Splitting of the Red Sea, we are not going to have joy over the fact that the Israelites were saved and the Egyptians were killed. This falsity has been perpetuated in the minds of Jews and non-Jews ever since. People believe that this is why we celebrate Passover but this is a corruption to conceal the opportunity that is available for all of humankind.

Time Travel to the Red Sea

We sing the *Berich Shemei* before we read from the Torah Scroll. This song acts as a time tunnel that allows us to travel back in time and tap into that awesome energy of mind over matter and be present at the Splitting of the Red Sea—a feat accomplished by the Israelites themselves as an example to the whole world. The sea did not just split at that location but also around the whole universe. Every body of water was split, and everyone everywhere participated in that.

Therefore, we teleport ourselves back to that time when the original Splitting of the Red Sea occurred. Those who are not ready to accept this are not obliged to do so. But why can so many not accept the idea that we can travel back and be present at the time of that experience; that we can take our consciousness and move it somewhere else? When we remember the vacation we took last year, we can go back to those memories in the flash of a moment. It works—just try it. There is no difficulty in doing that, is there? But still so many dispute the idea that we can teleport. To reject it outright is to succumb to our evil nature, the nature of Satan. We have been placed in this world to make sure we do not abandon it— to make sure we do not abandon the world to chaos.

The Battles Are Inside Us

Why did God need to kill the Egyptians when the Israelites had crossed the Red Sea? After all, were not the Egyptians also a part of Creation? Sometimes it seems that there is a battle, and we are victorious, yet the lesson is still that Satan never sleeps. We have battles that take place in the mind; all of us have mental wars, whether it is because we blame or get angry at others for what they have done to us, and so on. Satan creates these wars and he is with us all of the time, even though some days we have victories. We should not think that because we have a few successes the fight is over. Satan never gives up. He comes back again and again. Even though the Israelites crossed the sea and their enemies were destroyed, the next day they still had something to fear and something new to complain about.

The Zohar says that during the time of Rav Shimon, Satan complained to the Light. He said that no matter where he went

Rav Shimon caught him and triumphed over him. So Satan asked the Creator why he must keep doing his job. God answered, saying that this job is what Satan was created for.

Shemot 15:1 Then Moses and the Israelites will sing this song to the Lord: "I will sing to the Lord, for He is highly exalted. The horse and its rider He has hurled into the sea. 2 The Lord is my strength and my song; He has become my salvation. He is my God, and I will praise Him, my father's God, and I will exalt Him. 3 The Lord is a warrior; the Lord is His name. 4 Pharaoh's chariots and his army He has hurled into the sea. The best of Pharaoh's officers are drowned in the Red Sea. 5 The deep waters have covered them; they sank to the depths like a stone. 6 Your Right Hand, Lord, was majestic in power. Your Right Hand, Lord, shattered the enemy. 7 In the greatness of Your Majesty You threw down those who opposed You. You unleashed Your burning anger; it consumed them like stubble. 8 By the blast of Your Nostrils the waters piled up. The surging waters stood firm like a wall; the deep waters congealed in the heart of the sea. 9 The enemy boasted, 'I will pursue, I will overtake them. I will divide the spoils; I will gorge myself on them. I will draw my sword and my hand will destroy them.' 10 But You blew with Your Breath, and the sea covered them. They sank like lead in the mighty waters. 11 Who among the gods is like You, Lord? Who is like You—majestic in holiness, awesome in glory, working wonders? 12 You stretched out Your Right Hand and the earth swallowed them. 13 In Your unfailing love You will lead the people You have redeemed. In Your Strength You will guide

them to Your Holy Dwelling. 14 The nations will hear and tremble; anguish will grip the people of Philistia. 15 The chiefs of Edom will be terrified, the leaders of Moab will be seized with trembling, the people of Canaan will melt away; 16 terror and dread will fall upon them. By the power of Your Arm they will be as still as a stone—until Your people pass by, Lord, until the people You acquired pass by. 17 You will bring them in and plant them on the mountain of Your inheritance—the place, Lord, You made for Your Dwelling, the Sanctuary, Lord, Your Hands established. 18 The Lord will reign forever and ever." 19 When Pharaoh's horses, chariots and horsemen went into the sea, the Lord brought the waters of the sea back over them, but the Israelites walked through the sea on dry ground. 20 Then Miriam the prophetess, Aaron's sister, took a tambourine in her hand, and all the women followed her, with tambourines and dancing. 21 Miriam sang to them: "Sing to the Lord, for He is highly exalted. The horse and its rider He has hurled into the sea."

Song of the Sea

Most translations of Shemot 15:1 say, "they sang," but this is not what is written in the Torah Scroll. In the Torah it is written as *az yashir* (will sing), which is in the future tense—the translators clearly had another idea. "One word of the Torah," says the Zohar, "is the secret for all future generations." This is what it is all about.

These are not words of a song or a religion. This is the power that we need to overcome the force within us that says chaos should reign supreme. We come to a Kabbalah Centre's War Room to learn that we can overcome—that we can have dominion over chaos.

When we read the Torah Scroll you will hear it loud and clear. These words are transmitting-channels. Are we really interested in knowing how the telephone wires work or is it sufficient just to know that these wires are a means to take my voice to the ears of another person? This is what it is all about. I am opposed to translation of the Bible because the energy that can bring us mind over matter—control over water—is contained within the letters and words of the Torah Scroll. This is the secret. The *Az Yashir* (Song of the Sea) contains a strange combination of letters, which is not the usual method of writing the Torah. In it we see a collection of words with spaces between them, and then more letters with spaces between them. This pattern does not exist anywhere else in the Torah Scroll. This is the way Moses was instructed to write the scroll.

Az Yashir (Song of the Sea)

אָז יָשִׁיר מֹשֶׁה וּבְנֵי יִשְׂרָאֵל אֶת הַשִּׁירָה הַזֹּאת לַיהוָה וַיֹּאמְרוּ

לֵאמֹר סוּס אָשִׁירָה לַיהוָה כִּי גָאֹה גָּאָה

עֻזִּי וְזִמְרָת יָהּ וַיְהִי לִי וְרִכְבּוֹ רָמָה בַיָּם:

לִישׁוּעָה זֶה אֵלִי וְאַנְוֵהוּ אֱלֹהֵי

אָבִי וַאֲרֹמְמֶנְהוּ יְהוָה אִישׁ מִלְחָמָה יְהוָה

שְׁמוֹ: מַרְכְּבֹת פַּרְעֹה וְחֵילוֹ יָרָה בַיָּם וּמִבְחַר

שָׁלִשָׁיו טֻבְּעוּ בְיַם סוּף: תְּהֹמֹת יְכַסְיֻמוּ יָרְדוּ בִמְצוֹלֹת כְּמוֹ

אָבֶן: יְמִינְךָ יְהוָה נֶאְדָּרִי בַּכֹּחַ יְמִינְךָ

יְהוָה תִּרְעַץ אוֹיֵב וּבְרֹב גְּאוֹנְךָ תַּהֲרֹס

קָמֶיךָ תְּשַׁלַּח חֲרֹנְךָ יֹאכְלֵמוֹ כַּקַּשׁ: וּבְרוּחַ

אַפֶּיךָ נֶעֶרְמוּ מַיִם נִצְּבוּ כְמוֹ נֵד

נֹזְלִים קָפְאוּ תְהֹמֹת בְּלֶב יָם: אָמַר

אוֹיֵב אֶרְדֹּף אַשִּׂיג אֲחַלֵּק שָׁלָל תִּמְלָאֵמוֹ

נַפְשִׁי אָרִיק חַרְבִּי תּוֹרִישֵׁמוֹ יָדִי: נָשַׁפְתָּ

בְרוּחֲךָ כִּסָּמוֹ יָם צָלֲלוּ כַּעוֹפֶרֶת בְּמַיִם

אַדִּירִים: מִי כָמֹכָה בָּאֵלִם יְהוָה מִי

כָּמֹכָה נֶאְדָּר בַּקֹּדֶשׁ נוֹרָא תְהִלֹּת עֹשֵׂה

פֶלֶא: נָטִיתָ יְמִינְךָ תִּבְלָעֵמוֹ אָרֶץ: נָחִיתָ

בְחַסְדְּךָ עַם זוּ גָּאָלְתָּ נֵהַלְתָּ בְעָזְּךָ אֶל נְוֵה

קָדְשֶׁךָ: שָׁמְעוּ עַמִּים יִרְגָּזוּן חִיל

אָחַז יֹשְׁבֵי פְּלָשֶׁת: אָז נִבְהֲלוּ אַלּוּפֵי

אֱדוֹם אֵילֵי מוֹאָב יֹאחֲזֵמוֹ רָעַד נָמֹגוּ

כֹּל יֹשְׁבֵי כְנָעַן: תִּפֹּל עֲלֵיהֶם אֵימָתָה

וָפַחַד בִּגְדֹל זְרוֹעֲךָ יִדְּמוּ כָּאָבֶן עַד

יַעֲבֹר עַמְּךָ יְהוָה עַד יַעֲבֹר עַם זוּ

קָנִיתָ: תְּבִאֵמוֹ וְתִטָּעֵמוֹ בְּהַר נַחֲלָתְךָ מָכוֹן

לְשִׁבְתְּךָ פָּעַלְתָּ יְהוָה מִקְּדָשׁ אֲדֹנָי כּוֹנֲנוּ

יָדֶיךָ: יְהוָה יִמְלֹךְ לְעֹלָם וָעֶד: כִּי

בָא סוּס פַּרְעֹה בְּרִכְבּוֹ וּבְפָרָשָׁיו בַּיָּם וַיָּשֶׁב יְהוָה עֲלֵהֶם

אֶת מֵי הַיָּם וּבְנֵי יִשְׂרָאֵל הָלְכוּ בַיַּבָּשָׁה בְּתוֹךְ הַיָּם:

There is a universe that is flawless, and although this physical universe we experience is filled with chaos both universes are intermingled and thus connect with each other. As we mentioned previously, the combination of the Names of God, *Adonai* (*Alef, Dalet, Nun* and *Yud*), and the Tetragrammaton (*Yud, Hei, Vav* and *Hei*), which are numerically 26 and 65 respectively, collectively add up to 91, which indicates the blending and merging of the Flawless Universe with this chaotic world. The idea is not to make either one disappear, they are blended together. When the chaotic world blends in, suddenly it behaves like the Flawless Universe. This is the secret of the *Az Yashir*. It is the removal of chaos. The way to remove chaos is not by a gun or a scalpel.

We recite the *Az Yashir* every morning. When we come to the three words in Shemot 15:12—"earth swallowed them"—we scream them out and say *zaz mavet* (death run away), and then chaos removes itself. The kabbalists also provide us with another word in the 72 Names: the letter combination of *Nun, Yud, Tav*, (נ.י.ת), which is the Death of Death. There is only one methodology by which chaos will be consumed—and it is not by destroying another individual or creating more orphans and widows or sick people all around the world. No, chaos has to be swallowed up. We say *bilah hamavet laNetzach* (may death be swallowed up), may it disappear like the wind. We use the words "swallow up" because the only way we can remove chaos is by using a spiritual instrument designed to swallow it up. Physics teaches that energy is replaced—we move it from one place to another. This is what surgery is all about: take out the cancer and put it over there. But chaos in its myriad forms is swallowed up, never to be seen again when we use this instrument of the Bible. It is not a question of moving the chaos from one place to another, which is science's way. We are not moving it; it is swallowed up—and this is the only method. We need to take the chaos into ourselves but why do we want to swallow it up? Do we want to enjoy it? No, it is the only way we can control it. The concept is profound and we can comprehend it only to whatever level we are able to do so.

22 Then Moses led Israel from the Red Sea and they went into the Desert of Shur. For three days they traveled in the desert without finding water. 23 When they came to Marah, they could not drink its water because it was bitter. That is why its name is Marah. 24 So the people complained against Moses, saying, "What are we to drink?" 25 Then Moses cried out to the Lord, and the Lord showed him a piece of wood. He threw it into the water, and the water became sweet. There the Lord made a decree and a law for them, and there he tested them. 26 He said, "If you listen carefully to the voice of the Lord, your God, and do what is right in His Eyes, if you pay attention to His commands and keep all His decrees, I will not bring on you any of the diseases I brought on the Egyptians, for I am the Lord, who heals you." 27 Then they came to Elim, where there were twelve springs and seventy palm trees, and they camped there near the water.

A Mere Three Days

The Bible makes a point of saying that just three days later the Israelites had more problems. Three days is all Satan needs to put chaos into a mind where the awareness of a miracle has just taken place. It takes only three days until Satan can again overcome our consciousness. We know what the number three means—it means restriction.

Everything was great, and then three days later they had no water and they yelled to God, which teaches us that no matter what the miracles are, no matter how great their significance or how big the challenges may be, unfortunately we are always involved in a constant battle to control our own destiny.

After the miracle of the Splitting of the Red Sea, the Israelites came to a place where the water was bitter, so they called the place Marah, meaning "bitter." There they complained to Moses, and Moses again asked God for help—and another miracle occurred: Moses took a stick and threw it into the water and the water became sweet. Just three days earlier they saw that they had control over matter but they still cried for God's help.

Coupled with this little incident of the water at Marah, we have also the benefit, in Shemot 15:26, of the secret provided by Rav Isaac Luria, the Holy Ari of the four letter *Yuds*. This one verse, with its secret codes, is inserted into our daily prayers. God says, "All of the illnesses that I have placed in Egypt, I will not bring upon you, for I am the Lord your healer." What does this have to do with the miracles the Israelites experienced? It seems as if it is out of place but it is not. The Zohar says negativity is the source and root of all ailments, and if we treat only the symptoms, illness reoccurs. This portion contains a revelation through which we can remove illness and chaos, and convert its energy to heal instead of harm. Surgery that involves invasive procedures is not the best method for healing because we first suffer, and only then hope to be healed.

The root of all illness is our own negativity. That is why this verse is inserted here. The Israelites saw a miracle. They could do whatever they wanted—but three days passed and all was forgotten. This is how we are; if we think we are above this then we need a little more enlightenment.

Shemot 16:1 The whole Israelite community set out from Elim and came to the Desert
of Zin, which is between Elim and Sinai, on
the fifteenth day of the second month after
they had come out of Egypt. 2 In the desert
the whole community complained against
Moses and Aaron. 3 The Israelites said to
them, "If only we had died by the Lord's
hand in Egypt! There we sat around pots of
meat and ate all the bread we wanted, but you
have brought us out into this desert to starve
this entire assembly to death." 4 Then the
Lord said to Moses, "I will rain down bread
from heaven for you. The people are to go out
each day and gather enough for that day. In
this way I will test them and see whether they
will follow my instructions or not. 5 On the
sixth day they are to prepare what they bring
in, and that is to be twice as much as they
gather daily." 6 So Moses and Aaron said to
all the Israelites, "In the evening you will
know that it was the Lord who brought you
out of Egypt, 7 and in the morning you will
see the glory of the Lord, because He has
heard your complaining against Him. Who
are we that you should complain about us?"
8 Moses also said, "You will know that it was
the Lord when he gives you meat to eat in
the evening and all the bread you want in the
morning, because He has heard your complaining against Him. Who are we? You are
not complaining against us, but against the
Lord." 9 Then Moses told Aaron, "Say to the
entire Israelite community, 'Come before the

Lord, for He has heard your complaining.'"
10 While Aaron was speaking to the whole
Israelite community, they looked toward the
desert, and there was the glory of the Lord
appearing in the cloud. 11 The Lord said to
Moses, 12 "I have heard the complaining of
the Israelites. Tell them, 'At twilight you will
eat meat, and in the morning you will be filled
with bread. Then you will know that I am the
Lord your God.'" 13 That evening quail came
and covered the camp, and in the morning
there was a layer of dew around the camp. 14
When the dew was gone, thin flakes, thin like
frost on the ground, appeared on the desert
floor. 15 When the Israelites saw it, they said
to each other, "What is it?" For they did not
know what it was. Moses said to them, "It is
the bread the Lord has given you to eat. 16
This is what the Lord has commanded: 'Each
one is to gather as much as he needs. Take an
omer for each person you have in your tent.'"
17 The Israelites did as they were told; some
gathered much, some little. 18 And when they
measured it by the omer, he who gathered
much did not have too much, and he who
gathered little did not have too little. Each
one gathered as much as he needed. 19 Then
Moses said to them, "No one is to keep any
of it until morning." 20 However, some of
them didn't listen to Moses; they kept part
of it until morning, but it was full of worms
and began to smell. So Moses was angry with
them. 21 Each morning everyone gathered as
much as he needed and, when the sun grew

**hot, it melted. 22 On the sixth day, they gath-
ered twice as much—two omers for each
person—and the leaders of the community
came and reported this to Moses.**

Complaining Again

Only a few days after another transformation of the water, the
Israelites were complaining again. If we do not have bread, do we
cry to God to give it to us? The first thing they said was, "God, were
there no burial grounds in Egypt?" They complained that in Egypt
they had meat and chefs, and that they left all this behind, and now
they were brought into the wilderness to starve. These people did
not say, "Give me what I need," they said, "God, give me more."
We are always negotiating, we cannot be straight. We cannot just
be honest.

We then read about the *manna* that God created and that tasted
like steak to some, and like fish for others, or tasted like whatever
someone wanted, and yet the people still complained and
disbelieved God. What is the *manna* here to teach us? It shows us
what it is that is wrong with ourselves, which is the single reason
why chaos remains.

God instructed the Israelites only to take what they could eat—not
more than they needed for that day. They were starving, and got
angry at Moses. They did not believe God that the *manna* would
be given each day, and that on Friday they could take two portions
because on Shabbat there would not be any *manna*. So they
gobbled it up, and then hoarded all the leftover *manna* because it
might not come again tomorrow. And when the sun came up the
next day, the food had spoiled. Why would they want to listen to
God when, only two days earlier, God had showed them a miracle?

The Bible uses the words "the nation," not "a few people," went to gather the *manna*, indicating that this is about us and our own behavior. Even Moses became a little exasperated with the complaints of these people. How long is humankind going to behave this way? When will we realize that complaints originate only because of our inability to change things? If the Israelites then, and we today, have the ability to change things, then why are we complaining? Is it because we do not have what we want right now, or is it that we have forgotten? The Satan has got ahold of us. We need to remember that at the Splitting of the Red Sea, God told them, "I just gave you the tools—physical reality cannot cause chaos in your life." The Zohar says we should apply these tools.

23 He said to them, "This is what the Lord said: 'Tomorrow is to be a day of rest, a holy Sabbath to the Lord. So bake what you want to bake and cook what you want to cook. Save whatever is left and keep it until morning.'" 24 So they saved it until morning, as Moses commanded, and it did not spoil or stink. 25 "Eat it today," Moses said, "because today is a Sabbath to the Lord. You will not find any of it in the field today. 26 Six days you are to gather it, but on the seventh day, the Sabbath, there will not be any." 27 Nevertheless, some of the people went out on the seventh day to gather it, but they found none. 28 Then the Lord said to Moses, "How long will you re- fuse to keep My commands and My instruc- tions? 29 See how the Lord has given you the Sabbath; that is why on the sixth day He gives you bread for two days. Everyone is to stay where he is; no one is to go out on the seventh day." 30 So the people rested on the seventh day. 31 The people of Israel called the bread manna. It was white like coriander seed and tasted like wafers in honey. 32 Moses said, "This is what the Lord has command- ed: 'Take an omer of manna and keep it for the generations to come, so they can see the bread I gave you to eat in the desert when I brought you out of Egypt.'" 33 So Moses said to Aaron, "Take a jar and put a full omer of manna in it. Then place it before the Lord to be kept for the generations to come." 34 As the Lord commanded Moses, Aaron put the manna in front of the community, to be

kept. 35 The Israelites ate manna forty years, until they came to a land that was settled; they ate manna until they reached the border of Canaan. 36 And the omer is one tenth of an ephah.

Shemot 17:1 The whole Israelite community set out from the Desert of Zin, traveling from place to place as the Lord commanded. They camped at Rephidim, but there was no water for the people to drink. 2 So they quarreled with Moses and said, "Give us water to drink." Moses replied, "Why do you quarrel with me? Why do you test the Lord?" 3 But the people were thirsty for water there, and they grumbled against Moses. They said, "Why did you bring us up out of Egypt to make us and our children and livestock die of thirst?" 4 Then Moses cried out to the Lord, "What am I to do with these people? They are about to stone me!" 5 The Lord answered Moses, "Walk on ahead of the people. Take with you some of the elders of Israel and take in your hand the staff with which you struck the Nile, and go. 6 I will stand there before you by the rock at Horeb. Strike the rock, and water will come out of it for the people to drink." So Moses did this in the sight of the elders of Israel. 7 And he called the place Massah uMeribah because the Israelites quarreled and because they tested the Lord saying, "Is the Lord among us or not?"

Moses and Consciousness

In this section, the Israelites complained to Moses about a lack of water. This is a sad commentary on them but it is only here to teach us how easy it is to fall into the trap of Satan. I hear it all the time, and it pains me. Maybe this portion is here to bring a little remorse, pain and sorrow about what took place after this great feat was accomplished by the people themselves. After everything was said and done, they traveled three days and could not find water—it is always water.

So they came to complain to Moses: "Moses, do you want us to die because we have no water?" Three days after this amazing feat with water and again they were complaining about water. Moses did not respond. He could have said, "You split a sea and dried up the mud at its bottom, making a beautiful walking path through two mountains of water—and all with the 72 Names. Look at the accomplishments you participated in."

But Moses did not respond. Instead he cried to God, took out a stick, and there was water. There is so much emphasis on the idea of consciousness here. With this section we can understand what scripture wants to teach us, which is that if this wisdom does not work for you, and I cannot promise it will, but if you do not believe that in the end you will change physical chaos into the Flawless Universe, then we have all made a mistake in studying this material. This is the truth.

Without believing we can change physical chaos into the Flawless Universe then, tomorrow or the day after that, or sometime in the future, when you suddenly find your life in shreds, distorted, chaotic, and you throw up your hands and say, "How will I ever remove myself from this?", then know that this is exactly where you are—with the Israelites in that desert. If we know that whatever chaos surrounds us is an illusion—whether it is a physical obstruction, a tumor, or nuclear waste—we have to be prepared to remove it. We gain wisdom from this reading because of the blessed Rav Isaac Luria, the Lion of Safed (the Ari), who gave us so many secrets.

In these verses of Beshalach, we have the phrase "I am God, your healer," which is a blessing of the power of healing, and through it we are empowered. Before we can conclude the battle, God—the Lightforce—says, "I will put none of the illnesses that rained down upon Egypt among you." I have not heard of cemeteries closing or of hospitals shutting their doors. Nonetheless, here we are told that God will never again place upon His people these forms of chaos, as he did on the Egyptians. Why did God not keep his word? The answer is found in the question that God asked of Moses earlier in the story, "Why are you crying to Me?" We should not be asking, we should be *doing*.

If we meditate on the four letter *Yuds*, the Ari says, and include a person other than ourselves in our meditation, be assured that this person will receive healing. God does not say things He does not mean, and He does not lie. Rav Isaac Luria explains that with the 72 Names, and Shabbat, we have been given these instruments for healing.

Complaining and Removing Chaos

In Chapter 17, suddenly again there was no water to drink. The Israelites began quarrelling with Moses, saying that what he had done to them was a terrible thing. In demanding water to drink were they trying to prove that God was not going to do enough for them and thereby demonstrate that God does not exist? Were they trying to convince themselves that miracles cannot happen, that such things are too good to be true? Are we also busy with this dilemma day and night?

This time, though, they got a little more adamant. After all, how many times did they have to go through the experience of not having water? This time they included in their complaint that their children and all their cattle would die as well, not only themselves.

Moses asked God what he should do with the Israelites; he feared they would stone him because he took them out of Egypt against their will. Here again there is another miracle, and one performed by Moses himself. God said it is all water—this is the secret—and He instructs Moses to wave his staff and water will appear. Have you ever seen water come from a stone? No—but, in studying Kabbalah, we understand that it can. What came first, the water or the stone? Water was created first; water is Chesed, and stone is Malchut. Moses struck the stone and the entire nation drank the water.

Redemption will take us another thousand years if we continue with the consciousness of these Israelites. We are no different though— we are them. The minute a miracle happens, we are ready for the next onslaught of negativity. This portion is a lesson instructing us to avoid situations of this nature. The minute after good things happen to us, too often we ask, "What have you done for me today?" This is human nature. Chaos can appear in our lives countless times before we can achieve mastery over this physical universe but we should know that we are ultimately in control. What does discomfort matter if we know that the outcome will be for the best?

After all, the situations found in the Bible are not there to tell us stories. We are not concerned with what happened 3,400 years ago, and we are decidedly not interested in the complaints of these people. They are here to strengthen us. While we listen to the reading of these complaints, the Lightforce is coming through to strengthen us. The verses have no historical value; they are simply an instrument for teaching, a methodology to remove chaos.

The Essence of Water

In this portion we have read about three seemingly different and unrelated events: the Splitting of the Red Sea, the conversion of the bitter water at Marah into sweet water, and water that came out of a stone. What does scripture want to teach us here?

In the portion of Beresheet we read that on the first day of Creation the only thing created was water, which has the natural characteristic of Chesed (Mercy or sharing). Where then did Gevurah (Judgment) come from? It comes from Chesed, since Chesed is all there was on that first day. The saying "water seeks its own level" identifies this nature. Does water have consciousness? Our consciousness can be shown by the things we seek. Water was the first aspect of physical creation, and everything else that followed was created from and through water: the mountains, plants, animals, and humankind. Perhaps this is why our bodies are composed mainly of water? However, if water is the nature of sharing, Chesed, then how, at Marah, did the water seek to be bitter? Moreover, when the water emerged from the stone, it was not a miracle because even the stone itself came from water. Moses knew the system. Moses knew the 72 Names of God, and all the other Holy Names and combinations to manipulate all physicality in a positive way, and to draw water from the stone.

Because water is Chesed, the quality of mercy and sharing, it cannot produce negative results; it cannot cause drowning, for example. However, because of the sin of Adam and the time of Noah, water was polluted with negativity and no longer has that original essential characteristic.

8 Amalek came and attacked the Israelites at Rephidim. 9 Moses said to Joshua, "Choose some of our men and go out to fight Amalek. Tomorrow I will stand on top of the hill with the staff of God in my hands." 10 So Joshua did what Moses told him, to fight the Amalek, and Moses, Aaron and Hur went to the top of the hill. 11 As long as Moses held up his hands, the Israelites triumphed, but whenever he lowered his hands, Amalek triumphed. 12 When Moses' hands became heavy, they took a stone and put it under him and he sat on it. Aaron and Hur held his hands up—one on one side, one on the other—so that his hands remained steady till sunset. 13 So Joshua overcame Amalek and its people by sword. 14 Then the Lord said to Moses, "Write this on a scroll as something to be remembered and make sure that Joshua hears it, because I will completely blot out the memory of Amalek from under the heavens." 15 Moses built an altar and called it Adonai Nisi. 16 He said, "For hands were lifted up to the throne of the Lord. The Lord will be at war against Amalek from generation to generation."

The War with Amalek: A Battle with Doubt

Besides tapping into the incredible energy of the 72 Names of God, we also have a special section here on Amalek. The word *amalek* has the same numerical value as the Hebrew word *safek*, meaning "doubt," indicating that there is some hidden message for us herein.

This section of Amalek is only here to teach us—although it is not so clear without Kabbalah—that there is nothing of a physical nature over which we cannot exercise control. This kind of statement does not belong in our modern century because while scientists have an inkling that it is a possibility, there is no firm conviction that we can control physical reality. By virtue of the tools provided for us in this portion, we have the ability to control every aspect of the physical reality and thereby remove chaos from our lives. Through the kabbalistic tools we can make the physical world perform for us, thus making use of physicality to finally remove the chaos that originates in this physical dimension and turn it around. This is so profound that it would take me a long time to explain it fully. From a kabbalistic perspective, which is 25th century physics, we cannot remove chaos by cutting it out; chaos, in whatever form—a cancerous cell for example—needs to be converted and restored back into a normal healthy condition.

The question is what happens to all of these cells that sometimes suddenly disappear. I must say that we have had hundreds of cases where an X-ray taken one or two weeks earlier showed a cancerous condition, and the doctors were ready to operate four weeks hence, only to discover that the cancer is gone. The doctors, in these cases, say they must have made a mistake but it happens often. We kabbalists, however, know it is because we scan the Zohar and we apply the tools of this portion. We are not cutting out or eliminating chaos, we are converting it back to what it was before the sin of the Tree of Knowledge. Without the consciousness, the awareness that we cannot remove evil by destroying it or through war, we accomplish nothing. This is the secret of the portion of Beshalach and the 72 Names of God. This is where our power lies.

I doubt that many people have heard of the nation of Amalek historically. Scripture, on the other hand, says we should always remember what the Amalek did to us and never forget these people.

They were the first nation that waged war against the Israelites after they had left Egypt.

During the battle, when Moses raised his hands, the Israelites were victorious; but when his hands were lowered, Amalek would begin winning. Is this story rational? Did the two men holding up Moses' arms not get tired too? God said He would wipe out the memory of Amalek from under the Heavens. This does not make sense, though, because God also told the Israelites never to forget the nation that disappeared the moment this incident took place. Why should we never forget about Amalek? Should we also never forget about the Spanish Inquisition? The world seems to have forgotten, however. For most Jews today, the Inquisition never enters their consciousness. Even the Holocaust will someday only be remembered by those with a family member who was involved. Yet here is a conflict that happened 3,400 years ago, and we are supposed to remember it always?

The teaching here is not about the nation of Amalek. It is a metaphor. As previously stated, the word Amalek has the same numerical value as the word "doubt." In 1927, Satan grabbed hold of the minds of this world's most famous scientists and enlisted their efforts to destroy the one idea that could remove chaos. Satan is far greedier than all of us; he helped the scientists come to their conclusion that there is an Uncertainty Principle which rules the universe. This is the consciousness that we have come to battle.

At the Kabbalah Centres, we have come to establish a new existence, one where we say no to uncertainty. Certainty is something that we ourselves bring into reality. The truth is that with certainty—and this is an absolute possibility—we can control every aspect of nature and every aspect of chaos in this world.

Conclusion

Since the sin of the Tree of Knowledge, and unfortunately to this very day, the idea that chaos can be removed has all but disappeared. The opportunity to remove chaos was there for a few moments when the Israelites split the Red Sea.

We have made so many significant steps towards the removal of chaos from our lives, so I have to caution you all again, saying there is no question that if there is any reason we think this is too good to be true, it is then a major problem that we face. The nature of the human being is something that for millennia humankind has been unable to remove. There is only one blockage, and the removal of this blockage depends not on outside factors but is completely dependent on our own nature.

In this section, we learn that Pharaoh sent the Israelites out from Egypt. We also know that when they left they fulfilled their promise to Joseph to take his bones from Egypt to the land of Israel. Moses directed the people to fulfill that obligation, and they were led by the Shechinah with fire by night and cloud by day, which was a miracle. The cloud led them in the direction they were supposed to go, and it also indicated in which place they would rest.

Pharaoh said, of the children of Israel, that they were confined in the land; that the wilderness had locked them in. Rashi and the other commentators ask where Pharaoh was in all of this. Did he leave with the Israelites, was he also fleeing? This phrase does not mean that Pharaoh spoke to the children of Israel because that was a physical impossibility. As we have learned previously, the Zohar specifically states that not one word of the Bible can be altered because we do not understand the significance of even one letter. The Zohar explains that Pharaoh is a metaphor, representing that nature within us—that evil inclination—which can justify every action we deem to be correct, whether it be in its effect negative or positive.

Pharaoh decided to go after the Israelites, even after all that he had just been through. Was Pharaoh a wise man? He was Ramses of the Middle Kingdom, the man who controlled the entire world at that time—thus I would think he was at least as intelligent as we are today. So why would he want them back after being persecuted by the Ten Plagues? What did he want with the Israelites? Why not get rid of them? The Bible is teaching us about ourselves here. When the Israelites saw Pharaoh pursuing them, their immediate reaction was to state that they should have stayed in Egypt and died there at the hands of God. This is our nature, and the only thing that prevents the removal of chaos in our lives.

The Zohar talks about the time of *Ashrei* and *Oy*—the Age of Aquarius, which is here now—saying that it will be difficult to get humankind to release chaos. This means that when humankind will observe the miracles taking place in our lives, people outside will say, "It is a trick; it is too good to be true," and then they will dismiss it.

This is what we face now. Many people cannot accept miracles because, although they are true, it is not natural. They say that this is not the way things have been in the past, and therefore, since a pattern is there, it must continue forever.

The Israelites told Moses to stop with his nonsense and get away from them. They would have preferred to serve the Egyptians rather than die in the wilderness like abandoned animals. These are the words of the Bible. Moses assured them that they were going to see the miracles of God. This whole section makes no sense, and the reason it makes no sense is because this is not what the Bible means. The Bible stresses over and over again that there is a force within us that compels us to behave in a certain pattern of human nature, and that it is almost impossible to find a release from this force.

At the Red Sea, the children of Israel prayed to God. It is clear they had serious problems—the Egyptians were behind them, and the sea was in front of them. Here we encounter the familiar response from God: *Ma titzak elai?* "Why do you cry to Me?" I wish we could repeat these words of God's everywhere around the world. Whether in a church, a mosque or a synagogue, people all subscribe to what is written in the Bible. Why else would people be there if not to pray to God? This is why I make it clear that we have a War Room, not a synagogue. *Beit Knesset* does not mean a "house of prayer." These words have been terribly twisted so that they can conform to the view that this world has been based on for millennia.

The Zohar asks the same question, and responds by saying that the Israelites were given the tools by which they could completely remove chaos, including the chaos of death. The kabbalists were aware of this fact 3,400 years ago. Certainly, if someone who was not spiritual came up with this idea he would not be accused of being outlandish. In 1912, a very practical physicist and Nobel Prize winner said that immortality is possible. He said there is no reason why we cannot live forever. He said that the only reason we get old is because the cells do not receive the proper nutrients— meaning that the water surrounding the cells is polluted. The Zohar says God's position is that people have to take care of the removal of chaos—it is not His job.

God did not bring the Israelites, or us for that matter, into the world to abandon us. He gave us the tools by which we can fashion our own destiny. However, the Tree of Knowledge revealed another nature within humankind, the evil inclination—which seeks out the chaos that can bring doom to the individual. This inclination towards evil is what entices us to do certain actions we know to be wrong. We should be aware that it exists; it is a war we wage every day. If we are not aware of this evil inclination, we cannot make it. We are like a person sitting on the battlefield while bombs explode around them, thinking there is no war.

The reason why we come to hear the reading of the portion of Beshalach on Shabbat is to connect to the consciousness of the Israelites at the Splitting of the Red Sea, which was a state of mind over matter. As we approach the section with the 72 Names of God, in Shemot 14:19, 20 and 21, we have to program that computer of ours, the mind, to know that there is a phenomenon known as mind over matter—and through the 72 Names of God we can connect to it. At the Centres we know the construct of the 72 Names.

I have studied Torah from the age of three on, and even after hearing this portion read year after year, I was never made aware that there are three verses in this reading each containing 72 letters. I had never heard of it, and I would add that anyone not in touch with a Kabbalah Centre still remains ignorant of the significance and immense power of the 72 Names of God.

Each one of us must ask ourselves why we merit this knowledge that can remove chaos. We have all seen miracles, some more dramatic than others; our only impediment is doubt. I know personally that when we are of the consciousness of certainty we can get rid of chaos. We can be studying at a Centre for 20 years, but if we have not captured the consciousness of certainty, then chaos will still be in our life—that will not change.

We have become conscious of the Light, yet even after we have witnessed a miracle of some kind, the next day or the day after, when we suddenly find our lives in threads and have no idea how we will untangle them, we need to ask ourselves if it is because we have lost our certainty. If we know that whatever chaos is around us is an illusion, whether it is a physical obstruction, a tumor or nuclear waste, we have to be prepared to remove it.

The reason we cannot get rid of chaos, and why the Israelites could not keep it at bay, is because of our inability to maintain certainty. Certainty and chaos cannot co-exist. If we could keep our certainty, we would not fall into the grips of Satan. Try to keep your mind free of thoughts for more than one minute—it is much more difficult than you might think. If you cannot do it, then you have the same problem the Israelites did. We cannot keep certainty if we cannot maintain simple concentration.

In this portion the Israelites lost certainty even after all the miracles they had just experienced. So how can we, who have not seen the Ten Plagues or the Splitting of the Red Sea, maintain certainty? This is why we scream out the letters *Vav, Dalet, Alef* and *Yud*—*vadai* (certainty)—during the Morning Prayer. If we do not have certainty, forget it. If we think we cannot overcome those problems, then we never will. The War Room is not a place for relaxation.

About the Centres

Kabbalah is the deepest and most hidden meaning of the Torah or Bible. Through the ultimate knowledge and mystical practices of Kabbalah, one can reach the highest spiritual levels attainable. Although many people rely on belief, faith, and dogmas in pursuing the meaning of life, Kabbalists seek a spiritual connection with the Creator and the forces of the Creator, so that the strange becomes familiar, and faith becomes knowledge.

Throughout history, those who knew and practiced the Kabbalah were extremely careful in their dissemination of the knowledge because they knew the masses of mankind had not yet prepared for the ultimate truth of existence. Today, kabbalists know that it is not only proper but necessary to make the Kabbalah available to all who seek it.

The Research Centre of Kabbalah is an independent, non-profit institute founded in Israel in 1922. The Centre provides research, information, and assistance to those who seek the insights of Kabbalah. The Centre offers public lectures, classes, seminars, and excursions to mystical sites at branches in Israel and in the United States. Branches have been opened in Mexico, Montreal, Toronto, Paris, Hong Kong, and Taiwan.

Our courses and materials deal with the Zoharic understanding of each weekly portion of the Torah. Every facet of life is covered and other dimensions, hithertofore unknown, provide a deeper connection to a superior reality. Three important beginner courses cover such aspects as: Time, Space and Motion; Reincarnation, Marriage, Divorce; Kabbalistic Meditation; Limitation of the Five Senses; Illusion-Reality; Four Phases; Male and Female, Death, Sleep, Dreams; Food; and Shabbat.

Thousands of people have benefited from the Centre's activities, and the Centre's publishing of kabbalistic material continues to be the most comprehensive of its kind in the world, including translations in English, Hebrew, Russian, German, Portuguese, French, Spanish, Farsi (Persian).

Kabbalah can provide one with the true meaning of their being and the knowledge necessary for their ultimate benefit. It can show one spirituality that is beyond belief. The Research Centre of Kabbalah will continue to make available the Kabbalah to all those who seek it.

— Rav Berg, 1984

About The Zohar

The Zohar, the basic source of the Kabbalah, was authored two thousand years ago by Rabbi Shimon bar Yochai while hiding from the Romans in a cave in Peki'in for 13 years. It was later brought to light by Rabbi Moses de Leon in Spain, and further revealed through the Safed Kabbalists and the Lurianic system of Kabbalah.

The programs of the Research Centre of Kabbalah have been established to provide opportunities for learning, teaching, research, and demonstration of specialized knowledge drawn from the ageless wisdom of the Zohar and the Jewish sages. Long kept from the masses, today this knowledge of the Zohar and Kabbalah should be shared by all who seek to understand the deeper meaning of this spiritual heritage, and a deeper and more profound meaning of life. Modern science is only beginning to discover what our sages veiled in symbolism. This knowledge is of a very practical nature and can be applied daily for the betterment of our lives and of humankind.

Darkness cannot prevail in the presence of Light. Even a darkened room must respond to the lighting of a candle. As we share this moment together we are beginning to witness, and indeed some of us are already participating in, a people's revolution of enlightenment. The darkened clouds of strife and conflict will make their presence felt only as long as the Eternal Light remains concealed.

The Zohar now remains an ultimate, if not the only, solution to infusing the cosmos with the revealed Lightforce of the Creator. The Zohar is not a book about religion. Rather, the Zohar is concerned with the relationship between the unseen forces of the cosmos, the Lightforce, and the impact on humanity.

The Zohar promises that with the ushering in of the Age of Aquarius, the cosmos will become readily accessible to human understanding. It states that in the days of the Messiah "there will no longer be the necessity for one to request of his neighbor, teach me wisdom." (Zohar, Naso 9:65) "One day, they will no longer teach every man his neighbor and every man his brother, saying know the Lord. For they shall all know Me, from the youngest to the oldest of them." (Jeremiah 31:34)

We can, and must, regain dominion of our lives and environment. To achieve this objective, the Zohar provides us with an opportunity to transcend the crushing weight of universal negativity.

The daily perusing of the Zohar, without any attempt at translation or understanding will fill our consciousness with the Light, improving our well-being, and influencing all in our environment toward positive attitudes. Even the scanning of the Zohar by those unfamiliar with the Hebrew *Alef Bet* will accomplish the same result.

The connection that we establish through scanning the Zohar is one of unity with the Light of the Creator. The letters, even if we do not consciously know Hebrew or Aramaic, are the channels through which the connection is made and can be likened to dialing the right telephone number or typing in the right codes to run a computer program. The connection is established at the metaphysical level of our being and radiates into our physical plane of existence. But first there is the prerequisite of metaphysical "fixing." We have to consciously, through positive thought and actions, permit the immense power of the Zohar to radiate love, harmony, and peace into our lives for us to share with all humanity and the universe.

As we enter the years ahead, the Zohar will continue to be a people's book, striking a sympathetic chord in the hearts and minds of those who long for peace, truth, and relief from suffering. In the face of crises and catastrophe, the Zohar has the ability to resolve agonizing human afflictions by restoring each individual's relationship with the Lightforce of the Creator.

—Rav Berg, 1984

Kabbalah Centre Books

72 Names of God, The: Technology for the Soul

72 Names of God for Kids, The: A Treasury of Timeless Wisdom

72 Names of God Meditation Book, The

And You Shall Choose Life: An Essay on Kabbalah, the Purpose of Life, and Our True Spiritual Work

AstrologiK: Kabbalistic Astrology Guide for Children

Becoming Like God: Kabbalah and Our Ultimate Destiny

Beloved of My Soul: Letters of Our Master and Teacher Rav Yehuda Tzvi Brandwein to His Beloved Student Kabbalist Rav Berg

Consciousness and the Cosmos (previously Star Connection)

Days of Connection: A Guide to Kabbalah's Holidays and New Moons

Days of Power Part 1

Days of Power Part 2

Dialing God: Daily Connection Book

Education of a Kabbalist

Energy of the Hebrew Letters, The (previously Power of the Aleph Beth Vols. 1 and 2)

Fear is Not an Option

Finding the Light Through the Darkness: Inspirational Lessons Rooted in the Bible and the Zohar

God Wears Lipstick: Kabbalah for Women

Holy Grail, The: A Manifesto on the Zohar

If You Don't Like Your Life, Change It!: Using Kabbalah to Rewrite the Movie of Your Life

Immortality: The Inevitability of Eternal Life

Kabbalah Connection, The: Preparing the Soul For Pesach

Kabbalah for the Layman

Kabbalah Method, The: The Bridge Between Science and the Soul, Physics and Fulfillment, Quantum and the Creator

Kabbalah on the Sabbath: Elevating Our Soul to the Light

Kabbalah: The Power To Change Everything

Kabbalistic Astrology: And the Meaning of Our Lives

Kabbalistic Bible: Genesis

Kabbalistic Bible: Exodus

Kabbalistic Bible: Leviticus

Kabbalistic Bible: Numbers

Kabbalistic Bible: Deuteronomy

Light of Wisdom: On Wisdom, Life, and Eternity

Miracles, Mysteries, and Prayer Volume 1

Miracles, Mysteries, and Prayer Volume 2

Nano: Technology of Mind over Matter